Schöningh

EinFach
Englisch
Unterrichtsmodell

Mark Haddon

The Curious Incident of the Dog in the Night-Time

Edited by
Ulrike Breuer and Martina Peters-Hilger

Series Editor:
Hans Kröger

Einzelarbeit

Partnerarbeit

Gruppenarbeit

Unterrichtsgespräch

Schreibauftrag

Hausaufgabe

filmische Präsentation

Projekt, offene Aufgabe

kreative Aufgabe

szenisches Spiel, Rollenspiel

Vorwort

Der Titel der Reihe **EinFach Englisch** verdeutlicht Zielsetzung und Programm zugleich. Einerseits soll Schülerinnen und Schülern auf einfache Art und Weise der Zugang zu klassischen, aber auch neuen literarischen Werken und Filmen ermöglicht werden, andererseits sollen Lehrerinnen und Lehrern in der Praxis erprobte Unterrichtsmodelle angeboten werden, die die wichtigsten methodisch-didaktischen Ansätze ihres Faches Englisch abdecken. Dabei sind die Modelle direkt, ohne langes Einlesen einsetzbar und stellen Unterrichtsarbeit konkret vor. Als besonders hilfreich für die Praxis haben sich dabei folgende Aspekte erwiesen, die für die Gestaltung der Reihe wesentlich sind:

- Überblick über **Figurenkonstellation**, ggf. **Filmszenen** und **Inhalt**
- **Klausuren** mit **Erwartungshorizont**
- **Arbeitsblätter, Tafelbilder** und **Leitfragen** für den Unterricht
- **Piktogramme** als Hinweise auf **Unterrichts-** und **Arbeitsformen**

Das Prinzip der **„Components“** ermöglicht darüber hinaus den variablen Einsatz der Modelle in unterschiedlich konzipierten Unterrichtsreihen. Dabei stehen Machbarkeit und Praxisnähe stets im Vordergrund.

Das vorliegende Modell bezieht sich auf folgende Textausgabe: Mark Haddon, *The Curious Incident of the Dog in the Night-Time,* Cornelsen Verlag, Berlin 2008, ISBN 978-3-06-031117-0

Sprachliche Betreuung: Simone Duxbury-Ziemer

Fotos: S. 3: © STOCK4B; S. 10: © ullstein-iT; S. 59: © Cinetext Bildarchiv

www.schoeningh-schulbuch.de
Schöningh Verlag, Jühenplatz 1–3, 33098 Paderborn

Druck 6 5 4 / Jahr 2013 12 11 **Zweite, überarbeitete Auflage**
Die letzte Zahl bezeichnet das Jahr dieses Druckes.

Umschlaggestaltung: Jennifer Kirchhof
Druck und Bindung: Media-Print Informationstechnologie GmbH, Paderborn

ISBN 978-3-14-041252-0

Getting started

1. Describe the boy's facial expression and possible feelings.
2. What does the puzzle indicate?

Mark Haddon: *The Curious Incident of the Dog in the Night-Time*

Component 3: Solving two mysteries 50

Component 4: Christopher's journey 67

Component 5: Final reflections on the novel as a whole 92

Die Charaktere

Christopher Boone	Der jugendliche Erzähler lebt mit seinem Vater in Swindon, einer Kleinstadt in der Nähe von London. Er leidet unter dem *Asperger Syndrom,* einer Form von hoch-funktionalem *Autismus.* Während er in manchen Bereichen eine überdurchschnittliche Intelligenz aufweist, fürchtet er sich vor den Emotionen und Verhaltensweisen seiner Mitmenschen. Sicherheit empfindet er nur, wenn sein Leben in geordneten Bahnen verläuft. Sein Interesse an Detektivgeschichten lässt ihn seine Ängste überwinden, denn um den Mord an dem Pudel Wellington aufzuklären, muss er selbst zum Detektiv werden.
Ed Boone	Christophers alleinerziehender Vater arbeitet als selbstständiger Installateur. Seine Geduld mit Christopher wird auf eine harte Probe gestellt, als dieser trotz Ermahnung weiterhin Nachforschungen zu Wellingtons Tod in der Nachbarschaft durchführt. Er lässt Christopher in dem Glauben, die Mutter sei tot, und versteckt deren Briefe an den Sohn.
Judy Boone	Christophers Mutter hat ein Verhältnis mit dem Nachbarn Ed Shears und ist vor zwei Jahren mit diesem nach London gezogen. Sie versucht, den Kontakt zu ihrem Sohn durch Briefe aufrechtzuerhalten.
Siobhan	Christophers Lehrerin und Vertrauensperson hilft ihm, seine Erlebnisse in einem Buch festzuhalten.
Eileen Shears	Christophers Nachbarin und Besitzerin des Pudels Wellington hatte eine Zeit lang engen Kontakt zu Christopher und seinem Vater, nachdem ihr Mann sie verlassen hatte. Nach einem Streit hat sie sich jedoch von Christophers Vater distanziert.
Roger Shears	Der Ex-Mann von Eileen Shears hat ein Verhältnis mit Judy Boone und lebt jetzt mit ihr in London.
Mrs Alexander	Mit der älteren Dame, die in Christophers Nachbarschaft lebt, kommt Christopher im Laufe seiner „Ermittlungen" zu Wellingtons Tod ins Gespräch. Sie erzählt ihm von der Beziehung der Mutter zu Mr Shears.
Wellington	Der schwarze Pudel von Eileen Shears wurde im Vorgarten mit einer Mistgabel erstochen und von Christopher gefunden.

Der Inhalt

Der Teenager Christopher Boone lebt mit seinem Vater in Swindon. Seine Mutter ist seines Wissens vor zwei Jahren an einem Herzinfarkt gestorben. Christopher erschließt sich seine Umwelt, indem er durch Logik und mathematische Berechnungen geordnete Strukturen entwickelt, denn nur dann fühlt er sich sicher und geborgen. Er liebt Primzahlen, Hunde und rote Autos, die ihm einen Glückstag prophezeien. Neue Situationen und vor allem fremde Menschen machen ihm Angst. Besonders fürchtet er sich vor Emotionen und unberechenbaren Verhaltensweisen seiner Mitmenschen, da er diese oft nicht nachvollziehen und entsprechend darauf reagieren kann. Im Laufe seiner Ermittlungen zum Mord an Pudel Wellington beginnt Christopher ein Buch zu schreiben, in dem er seine Gedanken festhält, wobei er die Kapitel durch Primzahlen nummeriert.

Als Christopher kurz nach Mitternacht aus seinem Fenster schaut, sieht er den mit einer Mistgabel erstochenen Wellington im Vorgarten seiner Nachbarin Mrs Shears liegen. Erschrocken über diesen Mord, beschließt Christopher, genau wie sein Vorbild Sherlock Holmes als Detektiv den Mörder durch strategische Befragungen der Nachbarn zu ermitteln. Sobald sein Vater von seinen Nachforschungen erfährt, verbietet er ihm, weiterhin nach Wellingtons Mörder zu suchen. Christopher findet jedoch einen Weg, seine Nachforschungen fortzusetzen. Nachdem sein Vater seine Aufzeichnungen darüber gefunden hat, kommt es zum Streit, und der Vater nimmt ihm das Buch weg. Auf der Suche danach findet Christopher Briefe von seiner Mutter, die sein Vater vor ihm versteckt hielt. Dadurch wird ihm bewusst, dass seine Mutter nicht tot ist, sondern mit Mr Shears in London lebt. Für ihn bricht seine wohlgeordnete Welt zusammen. Das Geständnis des Vaters, Wellington getötet zu haben, führt bei Christopher zum Entschluss, zu seiner Mutter nach London zu gehen. Auf seiner Reise muss er sich vielen neuen Situationen und Herausforderungen stellen, die ihn zwingen, sich mit seiner Umgebung auseinanderzusetzen.

In London erkennt er, dass sein Leben mit seiner Mutter anders ist als in Swindon. Trotzdem lehnt er seinen Vater, der sich bemüht, sein Vertrauen zurückzugewinnen, weiterhin ab. So bleibt Christopher zunächst bei seiner Mutter und Mr Shears in London. Der Alltag mit ihrem Sohn ist für die Mutter und ihren Lebensgefährten jedoch sehr schwierig, und nach einem Streit verlässt seine Mutter Roger Shears und geht mit dem Jungen zurück nach Swindon. Auch hier gestaltet sich der Alltag für Christopher schwierig, denn die bestehenden Probleme und Hindernisse müssen überwunden werden. Geprägt durch seine Reise und seinen Erfolg, entwickelt Christopher schließlich neues Selbstvertrauen. Er hat sein Leben neu strukturiert und blickt optimistisch in die Zukunft.

Szenenübersicht

chapters/pages	contents
2 p. 5	The murder of Mrs Shears's poodle Wellington
3 pp. 6–7	Christopher John Francis Boone
5 p. 8	Mrs Shears's insinuations that Christopher killed her dog
7 pp. 7–10	Writing a murder mystery novel
11 pp. 11–12	Interrogation by the police officer and "white noise"
13 p. 13	Christopher's dislike of jokes
17 pp. 14–16	Reflections on the "Milky Way"
19 pp. 17–18	The meaning of prime numbers for Christopher
23 pp. 19–21	At the police station and how to escape
29 pp. 22–23	The name "Christopher" and his dislike of metaphors
31 pp. 24–26	Being let off with a caution
37 pp. 27–28	Lies and "proper novels"
41 pp. 29–30	Father's advice to stay out of trouble
43 pp. 31–32	Mother in hospital because of heart problems
47 pp. 33–35	Christopher's dream of becoming an astronaut and the beginning of Christopher's book
53 pp. 36–38	Father telling Christopher that his mother died of a heart attack
59 pp. 39–42	Christopher's decision to find out who killed Wellington
61 pp. 43–45	Reflections on dying, heaven, black holes and God
67 pp. 46–55	Detective work in Christopher's neighbourhood
71 pp. 56–58	Christopher's school and plans for the future
73 pp. 59–61	Christopher's "behavioural problems"
79 pp. 62–64	Father's order to stop the "detective game"
83 pp. 65–66	Dream of being in space with machines and computers instead of people
89 pp. 67–68	"Black" days in a row
97 pp. 69–76	Christopher's chat with Mrs Alexander
101 pp. 77–80	The advantages of maths in comparison with real life
103 pp. 81–85	Reflections on describing things when writing a book; description of the sky and alien spaceships
107 pp. 86–91	Sherlock Holmes and *The Hound of the Baskervilles*
109 pp. 92–93	Conversation between Christopher and Siobhan about his mother's affair with Mr Shears
113 pp. 94–97	Christopher's photographic memory
127 pp. 98–102	Father's discovery of Christopher's book
131 pp. 103–105	Reasons for Christopher's dislike of yellow and brown
137 pp. 106–108	Expedition to Twycross Zoo with his father
chapters/pages	**contents**

The author

Mark Haddon was born in Northampton in 1962.
After his studies in Oxford, he worked with mentally and physically disabled children and adults. During that period, he was an illustrator and cartoonist for numerous newspapers and magazines such as *The Guardian, The Spectator* and *The Sunday Telegraph.*
From 1997 to 1998, he spent a year in Boston, Massachusetts. Afterwards, he returned to England and started abstract painting, which he now regularly sells.
Since 1996, he has been involved in many TV projects and has won several awards, including two *BAFTAS*[1]s and *The Royal Television Society Best Children's Drama Award.*
He was also nominated for his 10th *BAFTA* for a BB● screenplay adaptation of Raymond Briggs's *Fungus and the Bogeyman* awarded in November 2005. Since 1987, when his first children's picture book *Gilbert's Gobstopper* was published, he has written and illustrated various children's books.
His first novel for older readers *The Curious Incident of the Dog in the Night-Time* has also been printed in a version for young adult readers. It soon became an international bestseller.
Today, Mark Haddon lives with his wife and son in Oxford, where he teaches creative writing for the *Arvon Foundation.*[2]

---

1 *British Academy of Film and Television Arts*

2 For more information on Mark Haddon, we suggest an article by Kate Kellaway called *Autistic differences,* published in *The Observer*, April 29th, 2003.

Vorüberlegungen zum Einsatz des Romans im Unterricht

Mark Haddons Roman, parallel für Kinder und Erwachsene herausgegeben, wurde bald nach seinem Erscheinen im Jahre 2003 zum Bestseller und erhielt gleich mehrere Preise, so den renommierten *Whitbread Book of the Year Award 2003* und den *Guardian Children's Prize.* 40 Länder erwarben die Übersetzungsrechte, *Warner Brothers* die Filmrechte. Bei *Vintage* wurde das Buch bereits in die Reihe *Vintage Future Classics* aufgenommen.

Das Buch ist hervorragend als Schullektüre geeignet, da es sprachlich leicht zugänglich ist, dem Sprachniveau bereits ab Klasse 10 angemessen. Gleichzeitig ist hervorzuheben, dass Haddon auf die Verwendung alterstypischer Jugendsprache, die immer orts- und zeitgebunden ist, glaubhaft verzichten konnte, da sich sein Protagonist, bedingt durch das *Asperger-Syndrom,* nicht in einem entsprechenden sozialen Kontext aufhält. *Four-letter words* kommen im Buch zwar vor, werden aber lediglich von Erwachsenen verwendet.

Die Mehrschichtigkeit von äußerer Handlung und innerem Erleben bietet vielfältige Zugänge und Interpretationsmöglichkeiten im Unterricht, sodass sich der Roman auch für eine Behandlung im Oberstufenunterricht sehr gut eignet. Die Hauptthematik des Textes, die Selbstfindung eines Jugendlichen, ist von zeitloser Relevanz.[1] Der Initiationstext ermöglicht sowohl Identifikation als auch Distanzierung.

Der Roman lässt sich in Unterrichtsreihen zu den folgenden Themenbereichen gut einbinden: *20th century novel, Crime, Young people in the adult world, Views of disturbed interpersonal relations, The individual and the group, Man in search of identity* und auch *Life in cities,* wenn man an die Wirkung des Großstadtdschungels London auf einen Menschen mit autistischen Zügen denkt.

In formaler Hinsicht lassen sich typische *elements of plot* narrativer Texte herausarbeiten, aber auch die sehr ungewöhnlichen Elemente dieses Romans (z. B. das Layout).

Da sich der Roman in zwei große, miteinander verbundene Sinnabschnitte einteilen lässt, und zwar die Detektivgeschichte und die Initiationsgeschichte, bietet es sich an, der Chronologie des Textes folgend, verschiedene Themen an jeweils neuen Abschnitten des Textes zu erarbeiten. Erfahrungsgemäß ist dieses Verfahren aus Schülersicht motivierender. Um ein effektives chronologisches Erarbeiten des Textes in größeren Sinneinheiten zu ermöglichen, können mithilfe von Arbeitsblättern gezielte Leseaufträge erteilt werden, die eine analytisch-interpretierende und/oder produktionsorientierte Bearbeitung der Einzelthemen im Unterricht vorstrukturieren.

Eine Vorablektüre dieses Romans mit einem Umfang von 259 Seiten ist alternativ ebenfalls denkbar. Dafür sprechen die von vielen Lesern als komisch empfundenen Passagen und auch die bereits im ersten (zweiten!) Kapitel des Buches entstehende Spannung einer typischen *detective story,* die einlädt, mit dem Protagonisten auf Spurensuche zu gehen. Auch bei der Behandlung des Romans als Ganzschrift können entsprechende Arbeitsblätter mit Textverweisen genutzt werden, um ein wiederholendes Lesen zu begleiten.

Zum Roman gibt es unseres Wissens bisher keine den Erfordernissen des Curriculums entsprechenden Unterrichtsmodelle.[2] Es sind verschiedene Ausgaben des Romans auf dem Markt. Diesem Unterrichtsmodell liegt die Cornelsen-Ausgabe aus der Reihe *Senior English Library* (ISBN: 978-3-06-031117-0) zugrunde. Es gibt mehrere Audiobook-Ausgaben, z. B. bei *Random House.*

---

[1] Der Klappentext der gebundenen deutschen Ausgabe (Blessing, 2003), Mark Haddon: *Supergute Tage oder Die sonderbare Welt des Christopher Boone,* zieht Parallelen zu J.D. Salingers Protagonisten Holden Caulfield aus *The Catcher in the Rye.*

[2] Patrice Floods *Unit Lesson Plan* (http://www.geocities.com/patricefl9481/unit.htm) bietet interessante Anregungen, verzichtet aber weitgehend auf eine Interpretation des Romans.

Klausuren

Im Folgenden werden drei Klausurvorschläge zum Roman gemacht.
Klausur 1 wurde Kapitel 229 (S. 233–235) zugrunde gelegt. Aufgrund der Textlänge (ca. 825 Wörter) ist diese Aufgabe eher für einen Leistungskurs geeignet.
Diese Klausur kann jederzeit im Laufe der Lektüre des Romans gestellt werden, sobald Christophers besondere Persönlichkeitsmerkmale angesprochen worden sind, und zwar auch ohne Einsichtnahme in den Roman während der Klausur.
Im Falle einer Vorablektüre besteht die Möglichkeit, die 1. Frage zu erweitern:

> 1. Briefly outline the context of this chapter and identify character traits typical of Christopher's mental condition that are apparent in this extract. *(Comprehension/Orientation/Context)*

Klausur 2 wurde ein Ausschnitt aus Kapitel 157 (S. 130–135) zugrunde gelegt. Kürzungen waren aufgrund der Wortzahl notwendig. Mit 592 Wörtern ist der gewählte Textausschnitt auch für einen Grundkurs gut zu bewältigen. Die Kürzungen betreffen detaillierte Schilderungen der Mutter vom Ausmaß der durch das *Asperger-Syndrom* bedingten Verhaltensauffälligkeiten ihres Sohnes.
Diese Klausur kann eingesetzt werden, sobald die bis zum Auftauchen der Briefe gültige Version des plötzlichen Verschwindens der Mutter (Herzprobleme, Krankenhausaufenthalt, plötzlicher Tod aufgrund von Herzinfarkt; vgl. Kapitel 43, 53) besprochen worden ist. Da sich die zweite Teilaufgabe auf sprachliche Aspekte der Briefe Mrs Boones bezieht, ist es sinnvoll, diese anhand eines anderen Briefes zu üben.
Sollte für den Bereich Evaluation die kreative Aufgabe gewählt werden, müssten den Schülern die Konventionen informeller Briefe ins Gedächtnis gerufen werden.

Klausur 3 geht auf die Erfordernisse des Lehrplanes im Bereich von *media literacy* ein: Da die geplante Filmversion von *curious incident* (Regie und Drehbuch Steven Cloves) zum Zeitpunkt der Entstehung dieses Unterrichtsmodells noch nicht vorlag, ist es möglich, einen anderen Film mit entsprechender Thematik (siehe Internetadressen) heranzuziehen. Gewählt wurden hier zwei Szenen des mehrfach prämierten Filmes *Rain Man* von Barry Levinson aus dem Jahre 1988. Ausschlaggebend für die Auswahl dieser Szenen war die große Ähnlichkeit des Verhaltens von Raymond Babbit, einem von Dustin Hoffman gespielten *Autisten,* mit Christopher Boone, wenn auch der Grad der Beeinträchtigung bei Babbit ungleich größer ist als bei Christopher.
Da die Gesamtdauer beider Szenen 7 Minuten, 27 Sekunden beträgt, ist es ratsam, den Abschnitt dreimal zu präsentieren und dafür gegebenenfalls zusätzliche Zeit (ca. 20 Minuten) einzukalkulieren.
Voraussetzung für den Einsatz dieser Klausur ist der Abschluss des Romans: Anders als Raymond im Film ist Christopher, wie der Schluss des Buches zeigt, in der Lage, allein zurechtzukommen. Aufgabe 3 erwartet eine Stellungnahme zur Frage, ob/wie man Menschen mit *Autismus* in die Gesellschaft integrieren kann. Als Vorbereitung dieses Aspektes wäre es zusätzlich sinnvoll, den Auszug aus dem Zeitungsartikel *How about not curing us* aus der *New York Times/Component 5* behandelt zu haben, da er diese Frage thematisiert: Eine generelle Lösung gibt es nicht, man muss sicher den Grad der Beeinträchtigung durch *Autismus* berücksichtigen, bevor man entscheidet, ob ein Individuum zu Hause oder aber in einem Heim besser aufgehoben sein könnte.
Frage 2 geht auf filmtechnische Besonderheiten ein. Das Thema Kameraarbeit sollte im Vorfeld bereits thematisiert worden sein.[1]

[1] z. B. anhand von http://jochen-lueders.de/vocab/film_analysis.pdf

Text: **Excerpts from *The Curious Incident of the Dog in the Night-Time* by Mark Haddon (chapter 229, "one of my favourite dreams", p. 233, l. 1–p. 235, l. 21) (about 825 words)**

Annotations

Blade Runner: a science-fiction film released in 1982, inspired by the Philip K. Dick novel *Do Androids Dream of Electric Sheep?*, dealing with advanced robot evolution in the 21st century: robots named "replicants" are practically identical to human beings, special police squads called "Blade Runner Units" have orders to shoot and kill any trespassing replicant upon detection/**PJ's Raspberry and Mango Smoothie**: a glass of freshly-blended tropical fruit (here: raspberry and mango)/**Gobi Aloo Sag**: an Indian dish (commonly called "Aloo Gobi" = a curry with potatoes and cauliflower)

Assignments

Read chapter 229 thoroughly.

1. Identify character traits typical of Christopher's mental condition that are apparent in this extract. *(Comprehension)*

or:

1. Briefly outline the context of this chapter and identify character traits typical of Christopher's mental condition that are apparent in this extract. *(Comprehension/Orientation/Context)*
2. Give examples of Christopher's use of contrast and repetition and describe their effects. *(Analysis)*
3. Referring to the extract above, explain to what extent you agree/disagree with the assessment made by Terry (a boy from school) that Christopher is a "spazzer"? *(Evaluation/Comment)*

Erwartungshorizont zu Klausur 1

zu 1: Christopher's character traits

Likes/Talents: being alone, isolated (cf. p. 233, ll. 19f.)/computer and computer games (cf. p. 233, ll. 5f., p. 234, ll. 8f., 20f., p. 235, l. 19); watching television and videos (cf. p. 233, l. 9, ll. 13f., p. 234, l. 22)/the colour red (cf. p. 234, l. 20, p. 235, ll. 17f.)/overacuteness of the senses, e.g. hearing (cf. p. 234, ll. 14ff.), observation (cf. p. 235, ll. 2ff.)/importance of maths and science in his life (cf. p. 235, ll. 9ff.) as a means to establish a certain kind of order/Dislikes: people (cf. p. 233, ll. 4f.)/being talked to (cf. p. 235, ll. 5f.)/France (cf. p. 234, ll. 11f.)/Problems: cannot understand facial expressions (cf. p. 233, ll. 6–8, ll. 19–21)/ inability to show compassion or any other feelings (cf. p. 233, ll. 15–18)/awkward behaviour (cf. p. 234, ll. 9–11)

zu 2: Contrast and repetition

- "one of my favorite dreams" (p. 233, l. 1), "in a dream you're allowed to do anything" (p. 234, ll. 25f.), "And then the dream is finished and I am happy." (p. 235, l. 21) ↔ within this framework of perfection Christopher describes a scenario with nightmarish visions, a world without any people, more comparable to a horror film in the eyes of most people, cf. hint at "Blade Runner" (p. 233, l. 14): "everyone on the earth is dead" (p. 233, l. 4, ll. 17f., p. 235, l. 7), "bodies of dead people everywhere" (p. 233, ll. 17f.), "no one left in the world" (p. 233, l. 19), a lethal "virus" (p. 233, ll. 5, 11), "infected person" (p. 233, l. 7), people "crash their cars or walk into the sea and drown" (p. 233, ll. 15f.)
- "there is rain pouring down" (p. 235, l. 3) ↔ "I take an ice cream from a shop and eat it" (p. 235, l. 4) = two things which do not seem to go together judged by common standards

  → contrasts hint at the fact that Christopher is different, "curious" (cf. title)
- **"And [...]"** (p. 233, ll. 1, 4, 6, 7, 11, 12, 14, 15, 16, 18, 20, p. 234, ll. 1, 2, 3, 5, 7, 10, 11, 13, 14, 15 ..., p. 235, ll. 1, 2, 3, 4, 5, 8, 9, 10 ...); all in all, the word "and" is used about 75 times in this extract (!) → Christopher is straightforward, he is not able to express himself or vary his words, limited vocabulary (of someone who attends a school for those with special needs) and linear sentence structure; to make matters worse, he hardly ever practises conversation, as he hates chatting with people and additionally, he is not in contact with other teenagers; moreover, he has many different thoughts in a row, there may be jumps from one idea to another; his thoughts are added like a chain
- **"I"**: the personal pronoun is used about 50 times in this extract → hint at his form of mental disorder/a form of autism (Greek prefix "autos" means "self")

zu 3: "spazzer"

- explanation of the meaning of the word (not entered in the OAD): neologism, most likely slang expression/teenage language/comparable to "spastic": an offensive word, sometimes used by children to mean "stupid", more generally handicapped person, idiot, lunatic, etc.
- pros: strange behaviour and extreme problems in real life (e.g. trip to London)/ cons: intelligence, especially with regard to science and maths/in one respect or another, very many people are different, should be seen as "special people" (p. 234, l. 1)/difficult to define what normal is/should minorities be disregarded or integrated into society?/German Basic Law against discrimination

zu 1: Context of this chapter (Ergänzung bei alternativer Aufgabenstellung)

- Christopher's father had killed Wellington and lied to Christopher that his mother was dead
- when he found out, Christopher decided to stay with his mother in London
- there is an argument between the parents over Christopher
- the dream helps Christopher to overcome the bad situation (escapism)

Text: Excerpts from *The Curious Incident of the Dog in the Night-Time* by Mark Haddon (chapter 157, extracts from one of Christopher's mother's letters, pp. 130–135)

Dear Christopher,

I said that I wanted to explain to you why I went away when I had the time to do it properly. Now I have lots of time. So I'm sitting here with this letter and the radio on and I'm going to try and explain.
I was not a very good mother, Christopher. Maybe if things had been different, maybe if you'd been differant, I might have been better at it. But that's just the way things turned out.
I'm not like your father. Your father is a much more pacient person. He just gets on with things and if things upset him he doesn't let it show. But that's not the way I am and there's nothing I can do to change that.

[... mother's early memories of some Christmas shopping, when her infant son started screaming and banging his head in an overcrowded shop]

And I remember that night I just cried and cried and cried and your father was really nice about it at first and he made you supper and he put you to bed and he said these things happen and it would be OK. But I said I couldn't take it anymore and eventually he got really cross and he told me I was being stupid and said I should pull myself together and I hit him, which was wrong, but I was so upset.
We had a lot of argumants like that. Because I often thought I couldn't take any more. And your father is really pacient but I'm not, I get cross, even though I don't mean too. And by the end we stopped talking to each other very much because we knew it would always end up in an argumant and it would go nowere. And I felt realy lonley.
And that was when I started spending lots of time with Roger. I mean obviously we had always spent lots of time with Roger and Eileen. But I started seeing Roger on his own because I could talk to him. He was the only person I could really talk to. And when I was with him I didn't feel lonley anymore.

Roger Mr Shears
Eileen Mrs Shears

[...]

And Roger told me that he and Eileen weren't in love with one another anymore, and they hadn't been in love with one another for a long time. Which meant that he was feeling lonely too. So we had a lot in common. And then we realized that we were in love with one another. And he suggested that I should leave your father and that we should move into a house together. But I said that I couldn't leave you and he was sad about that but he understood that you were realy important to me.

[...] mother's memories of a more recent argument with her son over his eating habits, which resulted in her toes being broken]

And I couldn't walk properly for a month, do you remember, and your father had to look after you. And I remember looking at the two of you and seeing you together and thinking how you were really differant with him. Much calmer. And you didn't shout at one another. And it made me so sad because it was like you didn't really need me at all. And somehow that was even worse than you and me arguing all the time because it was like I was invisible.
And I think that was when I realized you and your father were probably better off if I wasn't living in the house.

[...] *(592 words)*

Assignments

Read the passages thoroughly.

1. Identify the individual steps that led to the mother's decision to go away and explain the main implication of her version for the story so far. *(Comprehension)*
2. Show that Christopher's mother is not the most experienced letter writer, for example with regard to spelling, choice of words, syntax. *(Analysis)*
3. Comment on Mrs Boone's self-assessment "I was not a very good mother, Christopher." both from her husband's and your own point of view. *(Evaluation/Comment)*

or:

3. Imagine Christopher's father (Ed) had opened this letter. Write a letter to Mrs Boone (Judy) from Mr Boone's perspective. Here, you need to observe the conventions of informal letter writing. *(Evaluation/Recreation of Text)*

Erwartungshorizont zu Klausur 2

zu 1: The individual steps that led to the mother's decision

- the mother suffered as a result of her son's behaviour in public (cf. l. 13)
- in contrast to her, her husband was still able to remain patient (cf. ll. 14f.)
- when his attempts at calming her down had no effect, he lost patience (cf. l. 16) and insulted her, not taking her problems seriously any more (cf. ll. 16f.)
- Mrs Boone reacted to her husband's verbal violence with an act of physical violence (cf. l. 17), which became a kind of routine in their marriage (cf. l. 18)
- to avoid further marital rows, they stopped talking altogether (cf. ll. 20f.), which was why Mrs Boone felt isolated (cf. l. 21) and turned to their neighbour, Mr Shears, whom she could talk to (cf. ll. 22–25)
- several aspects finally paved the way for a new relationship between Mr Shears and Mrs Boone: his own unhappy marriage (cf. ll. 27–29) and the fact that her problems with Christopher got much worse, finally affecting her physical health as well (cf. ll. 34ff.)
- in the end, she became convinced that Christopher would be better off with his more patient father alone (cf. ll. 36ff.)

The main implication for the story so far

- obviously, the father lied to Christopher when he told him that his mother had had heart problems (ambiguous!) and died from a heart attack

zu 2: Spelling

- "differant"/"different": correct and incorrect spellings exist side by side (cf. ll. 5f.)/"pacient" (ll. 8, 19)/"argumants" (l. 18, cf. l. 21)/"nowere" (l. 21)/"realy" (ll. 21, 32)/"lonley" (ll. 21, 25), here again, the correct spelling of the word is also used (cf. l. 29)/"too" (l. 19) instead of "to", i. e. spelling problems even with regard to commonly used words

Choice of Words

- "cross" (ll. 16, 19) = colloquial expression/use of phrasal verbs: cf. "turned out" (l. 7), "gets on" (l. 8)/repeated use of the word "and" (ll. 3, 4, 9, 10, 13, 14, 15, 16, 17, 19, 20, 21, 22, 24, 27, 29, 30, 31, 35, 36, 37, 38, 39, 41), altogether 40 times in this short text, frequently also used at the beginning of sentences/moreover, limited use of other connectives, e.g. "but" (ll. 9, 23, 31) or "so" (ll. 3, 29), "Because" (l. 18)/limited vocabulary, cf. repetition of words: "things" (l. 9), "your father" (l. 8) instead of a relative clause, "weren't in love" (l. 27, cf. ll. 28, 29f.), i. e. long-winded way of explaining/"like" (ll. 38, 40) instead of "as if"

Syntax

- incomplete sentences (cf. ll. 18, 28f., 37)/easy sentence patterns, no subordinate clauses/lack of education or simplistic style because she wants to make herself fully understood by Christopher

zu 3: "not a very good mother"

- on the one hand: Christopher's mother left her teenage son, was not willing to put up with the situation any more/could have tried to call him or the people at school/ therefore, the letters can be seen as a means to ease her conscience
- on the other hand: it was not an easy decision for her to take this step, her reasoning is absolutely comprehensible/the reader feels with her/she saw that her husband could cope better with the situation and decided to leave/she has written one and sometimes two letters a week/still suffering from the situation, definitely

not a "refrigerator mother"[1] (cruel mother)/Mr Boone had no right to keep the mother's letters from his son/therefore, it might be asked in return whether Mr Boone is not a very good father

zu 3: Mr Boone's letter to his ex-wife (bei alternativer Aufgabenstellung)
ein Lösungsvorschlag im Unterrichtsmodell/*Component 3*

[1] Siehe *Component 2*/Some key people in the field *Research of autism*/vgl. dt. „Rabenmutter".

Film: Excerpts from *Rain Man*, directed by Barry Levinson (*United Artists*, 1988): scene 13 "Dibbs, Sally" (4.55 min), scene 14 "Toothpicks" (2.32 min)

Annotations

Rain Man is a Hollywood feature film and was awarded four *Oscars*.
plot synopsis: Located in a small town in the east of the USA (Cincinnatti), *Rain Man* is the story of two brothers, *high-level autistic* Raymond Babbit (Dustin Hoffman) and "normal" Charlie Babbit (Tom Cruise).
At the beginning, Charlie, a selfish yuppie and L.A. businessman, is convinced that he will be the sole inheritor of his father's huge fortune (3 million dollars), but he suddenly discovers that the money is meant to support his older brother Raymond, whom he did not even know he had. Raymond left the family and has lived in a mental home since little Charlie turned three.
Full of rage and with no consideration for his brother's mental condition, Charlie even kidnaps Raymond to get access to half of his father's money.
The two scenes that have been picked out take place in a roadside diner at the beginning of a cross-country road trip. This trip will eventually lead Charlie to an understanding and even love of his handicapped brother and to Raymond's return to the institution Wallbrook Home in the end.

Assignments

Watch the scenes closely.

1. Describe forms of behaviour that identify Raymond Babbit as an *autistic* grown-up and discuss aspects of his brother's nature that are revealed in these scenes. *(Comprehension)*
2. Analyse the director's camera work – concerning shots, camera position and camera movement – in this scene. *(Analysis)*
3. Answer the question of whether *autistic* people are better off in homes for those with special needs, considering the differences between Christopher and Raymond. *(Evaluation)*

Erwartungshorizont zu Klausur 3

zu 1: Forms of behaviour

at the beginning of scene 13, we see Ray and Charlie sitting at a table in a diner

- **Raymond:** looking off into the distance, avoiding eye contact, moving back and forth, murmuring something, without any particular facial expression
- being unable to maintain certain routines makes him anxious and upset (pancakes on Tuesdays/sugar, salt and pepper in a line/toothpicks on the table/maple syrup on the table before the pancakes are served, which seems weird, especially as they have not yet ordered at all)/his speech is limited to the repetition of short phrases/ unable to deviate from his expectations, cf. "definitely"
- example of his outstanding memory (automatically associates the waitress's name tag with her phone number/started learning the telephone book off by heart the night before)
- outstanding ability to do some quick mental arithmetic (scene 14: exact number of 246 toothpicks lying on the floor in a heap)
- all in all: obsessive tendencies in his behaviour
- **Charlie:** in scene 13, he quickly loses patience with his brother, shouts at Ray, gives him harsh orders, grabs him around the neck, hissing "Stop acting like a fucking retard!"
- becomes infuriated when he reads that Ray has taken down "squeezed and pulled and hurt my neck" in his diary under the headword "serious injuries"/not aware that people with autism abhor physical contact
- when talking to the director of Wallbrook, where Ray was institutionalized before Charlie came and kidnapped him, he repeatedly suggests a "deal"/typical of his cold business sense/the doctor's worries are "bullshit" to him/he is even willing to have a "custody battle" in court
- not very interested in other people/totally inexperienced with regard to autism; his sole interest is to get his share of his father's inheritance; he feels deprived of something which, according to his sense of justice, should have been given to him/his treatment of his brother in the two scenes is a good example of his initial egotism, selfishness, greed and ruthlessness; he does not see the human being in desperate need of professional help but instead treats the brother like a bargaining chip to get his share of his father's money/Charlie is not at all concerned about his brother's fate; kidnapping and blackmailing are used by him to achieve his aims quickly

zu 2: Camera work[1]

- **shots:** at the beginning, **long shot**, when the general setting of the scene (American diner) is shown, later again with regard to the interior of the diner/but mostly **medium shots**, showing the upper bodies of the persons and **close-ups** focussing on the entire heads of the persons to show their feeling/**POV shots** (point-of-view) are used to adopt the perspective of a character, for example, when Ray is looking at the name tag, or later on, at the toothpicks lying on the floor, in combination with **reaction shots**, e.g. the faces of the waitress and Charlie to show their amazement with regard to Ray's outstanding talents
- **camera positions:** mostly **eye-level shots**, where the camera is on the same level as the character/**high angle shot**: look at toothpicks from above

[1] Vgl. http://jochen-lueders.de/vocab/film_analysis.pdf

- **camera movements: panning shot** when Charlie is shown in the phone box and turns his head to follow Ray's movements

zu 3: better off in homes

individual answers, see newspaper article *Component 5, How about not 'curing' us, some autistics are pleading,* question 7

Konzeption des Unterrichtsmodells

Nach seinem rasanten, weltweiten Erfolg sollte der Roman *The Curious Incident of the Dog in the Night-Time* ebenfalls Eingang in den Englischunterricht unserer Schulen finden, und zwar entweder am Ende der Sekundarstufe I oder in der Sekundarstufe II.
Wie Christopher ist jeder Jugendliche mit Herausforderungen auf der Schwelle zum Erwachsenendasein konfrontiert. Der Roman vermittelt darüber hinaus dem jugendlichen wie dem erwachsenen Leser das Gefühl, dass die Grenzen zwischen normal und nicht normal fließend sind. Die Behandlung dieses Romans kann dazu beitragen, den Blick für vermeintliche Abweichungen von der Norm zu öffnen und Verständnis zu wecken.
Das vorliegende Unterrichtsmodell sieht ein schrittweises Erarbeiten des Romans in Sinnabschnitten vor:

1. *Getting started* (textexterner Einstieg)
2. *Christopher Boone and his little world of Swindon* (Kap. 2–59, S. 5–42)
3. *Solving two mysteries* (Kap. 61–167, S. 43–151)
4. *Christopher's journey* (Kap. 173–233, S. 152–256)
5. *Final reflections on the novel as a whole* (kapitelübergreifende Synthese)

Der Schwerpunkt der Interpretation liegt auf der besonderen Persönlichkeit Christophers und seinen Zukunftsperspektiven sowie der Reaktion der Außenwelt auf ihn. Darüber hinaus werden Besonderheiten der *detective story* und der *story of initiation* behandelt.
Die Reihenfolge der *Components* entspricht dem Verlauf des Romans und sollte beibehalten werden. Es besteht aber die Möglichkeit, unterschiedliche Akzente zu setzen.
Zu den Einzelaspekten der *Components* werden Arbeitsblätter bereitgestellt, die man variabel hinsichtlich der gewünschten Unterrichtsformen einsetzen kann.
Es empfiehlt sich, insbesondere aufgrund der unkonventionellen Form des Romans, den Schülern anzuraten, ein kapitelweises Lesetagebuch (Din-A5-Heft) zur besseren Orientierung zu führen, insbesondere hinsichtlich der Thematik und gestalterischen Besonderheiten des Romans:

Reading Log / Mark Haddon: *The Curious Incident of the Dog in the Night-Time*		
Chapter .../Page(s) .../topics dealt with	My personal impressions/ interpretations	Additional notes/ideas

Component 1 verfolgt das Ziel, den Schülerinnen und Schülern die Thematik *Asperger-Syndrom/Autismus* nahezubringen.
Component 2 behandelt den Romananfang, Christophers Persönlichkeitsmerkmale und die Reaktion seiner Umgebung auf ihn. Ein Glossar zum Thema *Asperger Syndrome* ist beigefügt.
Component 3 geht den Hintergründen des ermordeten Hundes der Nachbarin auf die Spur und beschäftigt sich mit den Ungereimtheiten beim plötzlichen Verschwinden der Mutter. Hierzu gibt es ein Glossar zum Themenbereich *detective stories.*
Component 4 begleitet Christopher auf seiner Entdeckungsreise nach London und zurück und stellt die Frage nach seinen Zukunftsperspektiven. Ergänzend findet sich ein Glossar zum Themenbereich *story of initiation.*
Component 5 rückt durch kapitelübergreifende Aspekte die Ganzschrift in den Vordergrund.
Abschweifungen bieten zahlreiche Möglichkeiten zu fächerübergreifendem Arbeiten, z. B.

- Mathematik (vgl. Kap. 101, S. 77–80; Appendix, S. 257–259) – mögliche Themen *Chaos Theory* (vgl. S. 123 f.), *The Prime Number Theorem* (vgl. S. 17 f.), *Conway's Soldiers* (vgl. S. 175 ff., bei uns bekannt als Solitaire-Spiel), *Monty Hall Problem* (vgl. S. 77 ff.),
- Biologie (vgl. Kap. 151, S. 123–126; Kap. 199, S. 196–197) – mögliches Thema *Concept of God's Creation versus Darwin's Theory of Evolution from a biologist's point of view,*
- Religion (vgl. Kap. 61, S. 43–45; Kap. 199, S. 196–197) – mögliches Thema *Concept of God's Creation versus Darwin's Theory of Evolution from a theologian's point of view.*

Weitere Referatthemen könnten aus den Bereichen *Asperger Syndrome* (vgl. z. B. Kap. 197, S. 189–195), *Detective Stories* (vgl. Kap. 107, S. 86–91; Kap. 139, S. 109–111), *Sir Arthur Conan Doyle's story "Silver Blaze"* sowie *Astronomy* (vgl. Kap. 173, S. 152–153) abgeleitet werden.

Component 1

Getting started

Der erste *Component* bietet verschiedene Einstiegsmöglichkeiten.

1.1 Talking about feelings

In einem ersten Schritt sollen die Schülerinnen und Schüler in Form eines *brainstorming* Vokabular zum Wortfeld *How a person might feel* an der Tafel sammeln, z. B. in Form einer *mind map.* Die Ideen können dann in einem zweiten Schritt geordnet werden, z. B. *negative feelings, positive feelings* etc.

Collect vocabulary that describes how a person might feel.

How a person might feel

bewildered, confused, curious, disgusted, happy, angry, depressed, apprehensive, insecure, sad, hopeful, scared, lost, frightened, frustrated, horrified, worried, pessimistic, nervous ...

With the help of the collected vocabulary, match the words to the emotions that are shown.

Im nächsten Arbeitsauftrag zeichnet der Lehrer verschiedene *Smileys* an die Tafel oder präsentiert sie auf Folie (vgl. Buch S. 6f.).
Die Schüler sollen anschließend die zuvor gesammelten Adjektive den dargestellten Emotionen zuordnen und erkennen, dass einige Emotionen leicht zu identifizieren sind, andere hingegen mehrdeutig sein können. Damit wird angedeutet, dass für Menschen mit *Asperger-Syndrom* wie Christopher, die Mimik nur schwer deuten können, die Deutung von Gesichtsausdrücken oft eine unlösbare Aufgabe darstellt. Das ist vor allem dann der Fall, wenn eine Aussage nur aufgrund der entsprechenden Mimik richtig interpretiert werden kann.

e.g. "Mary can't come to the party!" ☺ 😐 ☹

Now walk around the classroom and try to identify the facial expressions of the other students.
Give reasons why this is sometimes difficult.

1.2 Personality test – Take the *AQ Test*

Der folgende Test wurde vom Psychologen Simon Baron-Cohen am *Autism Research Centre* an der Universität von Cambridge nach 20-jähriger Beschäftigung mit dem Forschungsgebiet *Autismus* entwickelt.
Da nicht davon auszugehen ist, dass viele Schülerinnen und Schüler mit dem Begriff *Autismus* vertraut sein werden, lernen sie durch die Durchführung dieses Testes spielerisch einige Persönlichkeitsmerkmale kennen, die für *Autisten* typisch sind. Die Schüler werden feststellen, dass einige der aufgeführten Eigenschaften ihren eigenen entsprechen, die Grenzen also fließend sind.
Der Test *(Copy 1)* sollte jedem Schüler zu Beginn der Stunde vorgelegt werden, verbunden mit der Bitte, die Fragen wahrheitsgemäß und ohne Absprache untereinander auszufüllen. Um die Lerngruppe nicht in eine bestimmte Richtung zu lenken, ist es ratsam, die konkreten Informationen zum Test erst nach dessen Durchführung nachzureichen. Anschließend kann man den Auswertungsschlüssel vergrößert und auf Folie kopiert präsentieren.

The *AQ Test*

General information
- ➡ **Psychologist Simon Baron-Cohen** and his colleagues at
- ➡ **Cambridge's *Autism Research Centre*** created the
- ➡ ***Autism-Spectrum Quotient,*** or AQ = measure of the extent of *autistic* traits in adults

How to score
- ➡ **"Definitely agree"** (A) or "**Slightly agree"** (B) responses to questions 1, 2, 4, 5, 6, 7, 9, 12, 13, 16, 18, 19, 20, 21, 22, 23, 26, 33, 35, 39, 41, 42, 43, 45, 46 score **1 point**.
- ➡ **"Definitely disagree"** (D) or **"Slightly disagree"** (C) responses to questions 3, 8, 10, 11, 14, 15, 17, 24, 25, 27, 28, 29, 30, 31, 32, 34, 36, 37, 38, 40, 44, 47, 48, 49, 50 score **1 point**.
- ➡ **average score** in the control group was **16.4**
- ➡ 80 % of **those diagnosed with *autism*** or a related disorder scored **32** or higher
- ➡ test is **not** a means for making a diagnosis:
- ➡ many who score above 32 report no difficulty functioning in their everyday lives

Sicherlich interessant ist eine (von einem Schüler zu Hause durchgeführte) Gesamtauswertung der Lerngruppe ohne namentliche Zuordnung.
Es sollte der Hinweis erfolgen, dass es auf dem *autistischen* Spektrum verschiedene Ausprägungsgrade gibt, was im Laufe der Unterrichtsreihe noch deutlicher werden wird. Anschließend ergibt sich die Möglichkeit, anhand der Resultate ein Meinungsbild einzuholen.

Follow-up questions:
Is there anyone who would like to comment on his or her personal score?
Were you surprised at your personal score? Why? Why not?
Do you think we should evaluate the results of the group anonymously? What do you expect?
Does anybody already know anything about so-called *Autism* or *Asperger Syndrome?* Hans Asperger, a Viennese paediatrician, described children with *Asperger's* as "little professors". Have you ever had anybody in your form where this term might have been appropriate?

Personality test – Take the *AQ Test*

We all know that everyone is different, not only with regard to looks, but also with regard to character traits. The totality of your features, referred to as your **personality profile,** distinguishes you from very many other people.
In the following test, part of your personality is being tested.
Please answer the questions honestly, the results will not be shown to anybody else but you, unless you wish to talk about your score.
Once you have ticked off the answers which fit best, your teacher will tell you about the purpose and result of this test.

How to take the test:
For each question, record to what extent you agree or not and use the corresponding letter:

Definitely agree	Slightly agree	Slightly disagree	Definitely disagree
A	B	C	D

1. I prefer to do things with others rather than on my own.
2. I prefer to do things the same way over and over again.
3. If I try to imagine something, I find it very easy to create a picture in my mind.
4. I frequently get so strongly absorbed in one thing that I lose sight of other things.
5. I often notice small sounds when others do not.
6. I usually notice car number plates or similar strings of information.
7. Other people frequently tell me that what I've said is impolite, even though I think it is polite.
8. When I'm reading a story, I can easily imagine what the characters might look like.
9. I am fascinated by dates.
10. In a social group, I can easily keep track of several different people's conversations.
11. I find social situations easy.
12. I tend to notice details that others do not.
13. I would rather go to a library than to a party.
14. I find making up stories easy.
15. I find myself drawn more strongly to people than to things.
16. I tend to have very strong interests, which I get upset about if I can't pursue.
17. I enjoy social chitchat.
18. When I talk, it isn't always easy for others to get a word in edgewise *(= nicht zu Wort kommen).*
19. I am fascinated by numbers.
20. When I'm reading a story, I find it difficult to work out the characters' intentions.
21. I don't particularly enjoy reading fiction.
22. I find it hard to make new friends.
23. I notice patterns in things all the time.
24. I would rather go to the theatre than to a museum.
25. It does not upset me if my daily routine is disturbed.
26. I frequently find that I don't know how to keep a conversation going.
27. I find it easy to "read between the lines" when someone is talking to me.
28. I usually concentrate more on the whole picture, rather than on the small details.

29. I am not very good at remembering phone numbers.

30. I don't usually notice small changes in a situation or a person's appearance.

31. I know how to tell if someone listening to me is getting bored.

32. I find it easy to do more than one thing at once.

33. When I talk on the phone, I'm not sure when it's my turn to speak.

34. I enjoy doing things spontaneously.

35. I am often the last to understand the point of a joke.

36. I find it easy to work out what someone is thinking or feeling just by looking at their face.

37. If there is an interruption, I can switch back to what I was doing very quickly.

38. I am good at social chitchat.

39. People often tell me that I keep going on and on about the same thing.

40. When I was young, I used to enjoy playing games involving pretending (hier: *Rollenspiele machen*) with other children.

41. I like to collect information about categories of things (e.g. types of cars, birds, trains, plants).

42. I find it difficult to imagine what it would be like to be someone else.

43. I like to carefully plan any activities I participate in.

44. I enjoy social occasions.

45. I find it difficult to work out people's intentions.

46. New situations make me anxious.

47. I enjoy meeting new people.

48. I am a good diplomat.

49. I am not very good at remembering people's date of birth.

50. I find it very easy to play games with children that involve pretending.

WIRED Magazine – December 2001 – http://www.wired.com/wired/archive/9.12/aqtest.html

1.3 A poem

Das Gedicht von Dave Spicer, einem *autistischen* Autor, kann ergänzend zum *AQ-Test* eingesetzt werden *(Copy 2)*. Es reflektiert die Sicht eines frustrierten Erwachsenen, vielleicht eines verzweifelten Elternteils, der durch die Nähe eines *autistischen* Kindes überfordert wird.

Das Gedicht antizipiert die Haltung von Christophers Mutter hinsichtlich der hier zum Ausdruck gebrachten Gefühlspalette – Ärger, Verzweiflung, Verletzung – als auch deren Entscheidung, sich dieser Situation aufgrund von Überforderung zu entziehen.

Das Arbeitsblatt kann flexibel (z. B. Hausaufgabe, Klausur, etc.) eingesetzt werden.

Zu erwarten wären folgende Antworten:

1. the person speaking seems to be a grown-up, perhaps even the parent of a child with *Asperger's;* someone in charge of children with special needs would not lose patience so easily; very few people, if not parents, would voluntarily take care of a child like this on a permanent basis/<u>at present</u> the speaker seems to be at his wits' end, cf. "I give up" (l. 6), "What's the use of trying?" (l. 14), "I just can't take this any more" (l. 16), although he still feels the need to justify himself: "okay" (l. 6), "I mean" (l. 7)/the state he finds himself in is the end of many futile attempts <u>in the past</u>: "we tried to understand him" (l. 7), "Couldn't do it" (l. 8); he does not see any prospects for the <u>future</u>, either: "We never know what's going to happen" (l. 17), "but whadja expect" (l. 20)
2. on the one hand, the child seems to be very active and noisy: "He gets upset and runs off screaming" (l. 1), a condition which is even repeated at the very moment when the speaker seems to address the listener/reader personally: "Look – he's down there crying on the floor" (l. 15)/on the other hand, he is passive, introverted: "[he] sits there fish-eyed, dreaming" (l. 2), "he sits and stares at nothing" (ll. 4 f.)
3. the speaker, irritated as he is, does not beat about the bush when it comes to judging the behaviour just described: to him "that kid" (l. 4) can only be called "weird" (l. 4), "strange" (l. 9), he even uses the derogative term "pansy", which sounds contemptuous, and he does not hesitate to call the forms of behaviour experienced many times "crap" (l. 18)
4. the speaker seems to distinguish two worlds: "the world of men" (l. 19), to which the parents belong and which has a right to determine what is right or wrong: "we're right" (l. 11); in the speaker's eyes, their values and principles undoubtedly are the guideline/this seems to be reason enough to tell his son he had "better change" (l. 10), "learn to be a man" (l. 12) as opposed to the "pansy" mentioned above, "take [...] orders" (l. 13), "shape up" (l. 18), "grow up" (l. 19), "join the world of men" (l. 19) – the use of so many synonymous expressions shows how important this aim is to the parent. He seems to repeat this idea using different words in order to make himself fully understood. Alternatives are not considered, however, the last word of the poem being "THEM" (l. 20) shows clearly what little hope the

parent has that his son's situation might change; the son seems to belong to a different world, inaccessible to the parent (cf. "dreaming who knows what from who knows where", ll. 2f.)/the usage of capital letters is emphatic (cf. us versus them); parent and child have ended in a deadlock

5. the poem does not contain any hint at catalysts for the boy's behaviour, nor are alternatives for the boy mentioned, for example, a school for those with special needs; the same applies to changing the parents' handling of the situation
6. individual solutions

Dave Spicer: That Asperger Kid

He gets upset and runs off screaming –
that or sits there fish-eyed, dreaming
who knows what from who knows where –
so weird, that kid, he sits and stares
at nothing. Nothing! Every day
the same act. I give up, okay?

I mean, we tried to understand him.
Couldn't do it. Gotta hand him this –
he's good at being strange
he damn well better change
because we're right. No little pansy
any more, he's gonna learn to be a man
and take his orders ...
Now what? What's the use of trying?
Look – he's down there crying on the floor
I just can't take this any more.

We never know what's going to happen
wish he'd shape up, cut the crap and
grow up, join the world of men,
but whadja expect? he's one of THEM.

http://www.udel.edu/bkirby/asperger/dave_spicer_poems.html#That%20Asperger%20Kid

pansy coll. effeminate male, *"Waschlappen"*, *"Weichei"*

to shape up here: to improve one's behaviour
to cut the crap (sl.) to stop acting like a fool, *"mit der Scheiße aufhören"*

Annotations

Dave Spicer is a contemporary *autistic* writer (cf. http://bellsouthpwp.net/d/s/dspicer/)/**Asperger:** *Asperger Syndrome,* also called *Asperger's Syndrome, AS,* or the more common shorthand *Asperger's,* is a developmental disorder, and is commonly referred to as a form of high-functioning *autism.* In very broad terms, individuals with *Asperger's* have normal or above average intellectual capacity, with atypical or poorly developed social skills often with emotional/social development or integration happening later than usual as a result (cf. http://en.wikipedia.org/wiki/Asperger_Syndrome)

1. Who is speaking? What are/were the speaker's feelings (at present/in the past/with regard to the future)?
2. What forms of behaviour typical of the "Asperger kid" (headline) does the speaker mention?
3. What words/phrases reflect the speaker's attitude to these phenomena?
4. What solution does he suggest?
5. Can you think of any aspects not covered by the poem?
6. As an exercise, the author of this poem invites non-*autistic* readers to compose a poem written from the viewpoint of an *autistic* person. Give it a try.

Component 2

Christopher Boone and his little world of Swindon

Der zweite *Component* beschäftigt sich mit den Kapiteln 2–59 des Romans: Hier geht es um zwei Hauptaspekte, nämlich einmal darum, anhand der Ich-Erzählung die Persönlichkeitsmerkmale Christophers als eines jungen Menschen mit *Asperger-Syndrom* herauszuarbeiten. Ihm ist es unmöglich, Gefühle der ihn umgebenden Menschen zu deuten, er kann lediglich deren Reaktionen beschreiben. In einem zweiten Schritt wird die Welt um Christopher, vor allem die Reaktion von Menschen ohne *Asperger-Syndrom* auf ihn, exemplarisch näher beleuchtet.

2.1 A curious beginning of a book? (chapter 2)

In der Einstiegsstunde in den Roman soll den Schülerinnen und Schülern Gelegenheit gegeben werden, in einem *brainstorming* ihr eventuelles Wissen hinsichtlich der Kategorien fiktiver Wirklichkeitserstellung zu reaktivieren.

> Just imagine you wanted to write a novel yourself...
> What aspects need to be covered in the opening chapter?
> How would you try to grab the reader's interest?
> Think of novels you read in the past. How were the first pages made interesting?

Während der anschließenden Sammelphase können die Ideen an der Tafel festgehalten werden und nach einer Lektüre des Eingangskapitels die genannten Kriterien provisorisch auf diesen Buchanfang angewendet werden:

> What do we actually get to know here?
> Read the chapter again silently. This time you should read between the lines to find out as much as possible.

Die Ergebnisse der dann folgenden detaillierten Analyse können mithilfe eines auf Folie kopierten Rasters *(Copy 3)* systematisch erarbeitet werden. Neben der reinen Informationsentnahme wird der Blick dafür geschärft, dass Christophers Schilderung des Vorfalls mehr über ihn aussagt, als man zunächst annehmen würde. Im Unterrichtsgespräch folgt dann die abschließende Wertung.

> Does Haddon manage to arouse the reader's interest so that he or she wants to learn more?
> The title of the book is *The Curious Incident of the Dog in the Night-Time.* Is there anything curious yet? (hier: *"curious"* = kurios, seltsam!)
> What questions might come up now that you have analysed chapter 2 in detail?
> Describe the overall effect of this beginning on you.

Zu erwarten wären hier folgende Fragen:

> Why is the first chapter of the book called chapter 2?
> Who killed the dog?
> Why was the dog killed at all?
> Why was it killed so brutally?
> Why does the boy react so strangely upon finding the dog?
> Why is the boy walking around in the middle of the night in the first place instead of lying in bed asleep?
> What is the boy doing outside another person's house at 12.07 a.m.?
> Where are his parents?
> Why does the novel start with a dead dog instead of a dead human being as is usual in most other murder mystery novels?
> What aspects will the novel focus on more, the question "who had killed him" or the story of the "wonderer"?

Die allgemeine Wirkung des Kapitels könnte wie folgt beschrieben werden:

> On the one hand, chapter 2 may create a darkly comic image of a dead dog pinned to the ground by a gardening fork. The comic effect is achieved by the stark contrast of the brutal deed and the emotionless reasoning of the boy.
> On the other hand, readers may simply feel with the boy, who has obviously lost an animal he liked. They might ask themselves, however, why the boy does not show any "normal" reactions such as crying, running away from this unpleasant sight, telling his parents right away, etc.

Je nach verbliebener Zeit kann man auf die Formulierung der Überschrift eingehen:

> What does "incident" mean?
> What is unusual about the choice of words here?
> What other words instead of "incident" might have been used?

Hier könnte den Schülern bereits bewusst werden, dass sich Christophers Wortwahl von der eines Teenagers seines Alters abhebt. Folgende Antwort ist hier denkbar:

> An "incident" is something that happens, especially something unusual or unpleasant. The word can, moreover, hint at a serious or violent event such as a crime. Christopher's choice of words is different from normal teenage language. The word "incident" sounds more elegant, refined or polished than "killing", "murder", etc., which most teenagers might have used instead.

Als zusammenfassende Hausaufgabe könnte auf der Grundlage der erarbeiteten Ergebnisse folgender Schreibauftrag erteilt werden:

> Is this kind of beginning convincing as you see it? Give reasons.

Bei einem schrittweisen Erarbeiten des Romans ist ein vorbereitender Arbeitsauftrag zu den folgenden Themenbereichen, *Christopher John Francis Boone – A character portrayal* (siehe 2.2) sowie *Christopher and the police* (siehe 2.3), sinnvoll im Interesse einer textgestützten Erarbeitung der Kapitel 3–59, S. 6–42.

The opening situation: A curious beginning? (chapter 2)

Please read the chapter intensively.
Complete the column "what the text says …" on your own.
Try and find as many clues as possible.
Then discuss the meaning of your findings with your partner and add notes under "what it means …".
The last column "anything curious" will be dealt with in class.

wh-questions	elements	what the text says ...	what it means ...	anything "curious"
when?	time			
where?	place			
who?	characters/ main character = protagonist minor character			
what?	action			
why?	conflict/ external internal			

Lösungsvorschlag zu *Copy 3:*

wh-questions	elements	what the text says ...	what it means ...	anything "curious"
when?	**time**	"it was 7 minutes after midnight" (p. 5, l. 1)	dark, in the middle of the night	unusually precise statement, scary
where?	**place**	"in the middle of the lawn in front of Mrs Shears' house" (p. 5, ll. 1 f.)	ordinary neighbourhood, suburb? detached house?	nothing special
who?	**characters/ main character = protagonist**	• "I decided" (p. 5, l. 7) • "I could not see" (l. 8) • "I do not think" (l. 9) • "I could not be certain about this" (l. 12) • "I went through Mrs Shears' gate, closing it behind me. I walked down onto her lawn and knelt beside the dog. I put my hand on the muzzle of the dog." (p. 5, ll. 13 ff.) • "I stroked Wellington." (p. 5, l. 23)	• 1st person narrator • verbs of perception • uses his mind • observes closely • pays attention to details • no panic reaction • calm way of dealing with a scary situation • not disgusted, but even prepared to touch the dead animal • likes the dog • names the first chapter: chapter 2	• excellent in logical reasoning/perhaps not a typical 15-year old? • strange, inexplicable
	minor character	Mrs Shears = • owner of the dead dog (cf. p. 5, ll. 16 f.), next door neighbour (cf. p. 5, ll. 17 f.) • "who was our friend" (p. 5, l. 17)		
what?	**action**	protagonist finds killed dog named Wellington in neighbour's garden		gardening fork – brutal, cruel way of killing an animal
why?	**conflict/ external internal**	• "I wondered who had killed him, and why." (p. 5, l. 23)	• "who": possibly external conflict between the "killer" and Christopher • "wondered": possibly internal conflict inside of Christopher	

2.2 Christopher John Francis Boone – A character portrayal (chapters 3–59)

Als vorbereitende Hausaufgabe zum Thema dient folgender Arbeitsauftrag:

> Mark passages which will enable us to talk about Christopher's nature in the following lesson, particularly his likes, dislikes and problems that he is confronted with.

Um das komplexe Phänomen des *Asperger-Syndroms* systematischer begreifen zu können, empfehlen wir den Einsatz des Arbeitsblattes zu *While-reading activities (Copy 4*/drei Gruppen von ca. 4–5 Leuten, arbeitsteiliges Vorgehen/alternativ: je 2 arbeitsgleiche Teilgruppen bei größeren Kursstärken). In der folgenden Unterrichtsstunde erfolgt innerhalb der Gruppen eine Besprechung der Teilresultate und anschließend eine Präsentation der endgültigen Ergebnisse unter Einbeziehung aller Gruppenteilnehmer. Während der Vorträge sollten von den Zuhörenden Notizen angefertigt werden.
Zusätzlich kann danach zur Festigung die Zusammenfassung *The Triad of Impairments* der *National Autistic Society* (http://www.nas.org.uk/nas/jsp/polopoly.jsp?d=458&a=5489) auf Folie präsentiert und von Schülern erläutert werden.
An dieser Stelle ist ein Exkurs bezüglich der Erzählperspektive möglich.[1] Dieser zeigt, dass Haddon die Illusion eines autistischen Autors – Christopher scheint seine persönliche Geschichte zu schildern – erweckt. In diesem Zusammenhang kann der im Jahre 1961 geprägte Begriff *unreliable narrator* des Literaturkritikers Wayne C. Booth aus seinem Werk *The Rhetoric of Fiction* eingeführt und die Frage seiner Relevanz für Haddons Roman diskutiert werden.

Wayne Booth: *The Rhetoric of Fiction (1961)*

Unreliable narrator: The credibility of the narrator, either first-person or third-person, is seriously compromised. This unreliability can be due to psychological instability or other disability, a powerful bias, a lack of knowledge, or even a deliberate attempt to deceive the reader/audience.

> To what extent is this term applicable to the novel?

Zu erwarten sind folgende Antworten:

> **Applicable:** Point of view = **first-person narrative** (= a literary technique in which the story is narrated by a character who refers to himself in the first person, i. e. "I"); normally the first-person narrator expresses his feelings, too, which Christopher due to *Asperger's* cannot; he also takes every statement at face value/cannot understand figurative meanings, which often contributes to the humorous effect of many passages and

[1] „Und wo, bitte, bleibt der Autor? Mark Haddon verschwindet […] hinter seinem Helden, der das Chaos in und um sich herum protokolliert, als sei er autonom. Das spricht für die Empathie Haddons, der nirgends den Eindruck entstehen lässt, die Dramatik der Geschichte sei inszeniert." (DIE ZEIT, http://www.zeit.de/2004/08/KJ-Haddon)

gives the impression that the story is authentic, i. e. told by a person with *Asperger's.*
Not applicable: At the same time, Christopher is very reliable, despite these deficits; hardly anyone could describe things/events more precisely than he does, as he cannot distinguish important from unimportant.

Es kann einem Schülerteam der Langzeitauftrag erteilt werden, im weiteren Verlauf der Unterrichtsreihe das Thema *The illusion of an autistic author zu* verfolgen.

As you read on, mark all the passages where Mark Haddon conveys the impression that the novel was written by Christopher himself.
You may want to consider contents/structure/layout.

Zu erwarten sind folgende Ergebnisse:

- contents: **little professor**/examples of **mathematical virtuosity** and **interest in science** and **mystery** throughout the book – e.g. prime numbers (cf. pp. 17 f.), equations (cf. pp. 192, 194, 257 ff.), Milky Way (cf. pp. 14 ff.), Minesweeper (cf. pp. 30, 244), space (cf. pp. 65 f., 144), Monty Hall Problem (cf. pp. 77 ff.), scientific names of animals (cf. p. 106), Cottingley Fairies (cf. pp. 109 ff.), Greek, Latin and other foreign terms (cf. pp. 23, 98, 210), hint at James Gleick's Chaos Theory (cf. p. 117), hint at TV series *How the Mind Works* (cf. p. 143), constellations (cf. pp. 152 f.), Conway's Soldiers (cf. pp. 175 ff.), science books (cf. pp. 241, 256), *The Blue Planet* videos (cf. p. 245), hint at magazine *The Unexplained* (= quarterly print publication that features articles on ancient mysteries, true ghost stories, etc., cf. p. 110)/**book worm/familiarity with literature** – e.g. Arthur Conan Doyle (cf. pp. 10, 86–91, 110, 158 f., 162), Joseph Conrad (cf. p. 67), hint at *The Strand* magazine (= leading monthly fiction magazine, published Sherlock Holmes stories, cf. p. 110)/illustration of a situation in his brain comparable to a computer crash (cf. pp. 201 f.)
- structure: **digressions/lack of coherence among several chapters** (vgl. Lösungsvorschläge zu *Copy 4*, "cohesive story telling")
- layout: **illustrations** (all in all, about 40, showing maps, timetables, signs, patterns, animals etc.)

Als Übergang zur nächsten Sequenz ist folgende Aufgabe geeignet:

Now we have learned a lot about Christopher's character and special features.
If you were the director of a film and had the task of finding a suitable young man from the real world, either a celebrity or an ordinary boy, who would you pick out?
At home, have a look at magazines, newspapers, etc. or use the internet to find someone who best represents Christopher.
At school, you will have to present the picture and give reasons for your choice.

In der nächsten Stunde erfolgt die Auswertung:

Which of the pictures shown is the best choice? Why? Give reasons, referring to the book.

Eine Erweiterung des Themenbereiches *Asperger-Syndrom/Autismus* kann in Referatform nach folgender Struktur und dem *word field Asperger Syndrome (Copy 5)* erfolgen.

Some key people in the field *"Research on autism"*
Try and find information on the internet.

name	**dates of life/profes-sion/place of work/ special features of biography**	**object of research**	**major publica-tion(s) related to *autism***	**definition/ explanation of *autism***
Dr. Leo Kanner				
Dr. Hans Asperger and Dr. Lorna Wing				
Dr. Bruno Bettelheim				
Dr. Bernard Rimland				

Folgendes Ergebnis ist zu erwarten:

name	**dates of life/ profession/ place of work/ special features of biography**	**object of research**	**major publica-tion(s) related to *autism***	**definition/ explanation of *autism***
Dr. Leo Kanner	1894–1981 child psychia-trist and physician/John Hopkins University, Baltimore (USA)	description of the behaviour of 11 *autistic* children	1943 *Autistic Disturbances of Affective Contact*	coined word *autism* (Greek *auto = self)* referring to children who seemed to be living in a "shell" within themselves/ biology impor-tant, i.e. children born with this inability

name	dates of life/ profession/ place of work/ special features of biography	object of research	major publication(s) related to *autism*	definition/ explanation of *autism*
Dr. Hans Asperger	1906–1980 paediatrician/ University of Vienna (Austria)	study of 200 families with *autistic* children	1944 article *Die Autistischen Psychopathen im Kindesalter,* translated into English in 1989	described features of "little professors"
Dr. Lorna Wing	psychiatrist and physician (GB)/1962 founder of the *National Autistic Society*	mother of an *autistic* daughter	1981 *Asperger Syndrome: A Clinical Account*	introduced the term *Asperger's Syndrome*
Dr. Bruno Bettelheim	1903–1990 Austrian, Jewish, survivor of Nazi concentration camps, emigrated to the USA/art historian/later director of the *Orthogenic School* (home for disturbed children/ University of Chicago)	drew parallels between children with *autism* and those interned in the Nazi concentration camps and between the mothers of children with *autism* and SS guards	1967 best-selling book *The Empty Fortress. Infantile Autism and the Birth of Self*	coined the term "refrigerator mothers", i. e. cold and emotionally distant mothers who cause *autism* (not accepted as a scientific explanation anymore)
Dr. Bernard Rimland	*1928 psychologist (USA)/founder of the *Autism Society of America*	father of a son with *autism*	1964 *Infantile Autism*	opposed Bettelheim's thesis, *autism* = neurological disorder

Christopher John Francis Boone – A character portrayal While-reading activities (chapters 3–59)

At home, read chapters 3–59 of the book and do the following while-reading activities.

1. All groups: In the book, mark Christopher's **likes** and **dislikes** with the following symbols. ☺ ☹

2. Additionally, you need to specialize in one of the following topics, **by making notes and marking passages. Remember, however, to make sure that you give text evidence any time you take something down.**

Group 1: Pay special attention to **Christopher's social relations.**

The following questions may help you to do this task:

How does he **interact** with others?
To what extent does he act according to **social rules**? Does he observe, ignore or break social rules? Give examples.
What **friends/acquaintances** does he have? What people are around him?
To what extent does he respond to **peer-group pressure** (peer group = a group of people of the same age and social status)?
What do other **people's emotions** mean to Christopher?

Group 2: Have a close look at **Christopher's language and communication.**

Consider the following aspects in particular:

How advanced or minimal are Christopher's **communication skills**? Give examples.
Can he generally engage in **routine social interactions** such as greeting, etc.?
How large is his **vocabulary** with regard to general topics and with regard to specific areas?
Comment on his **sentence structure**.
Is he able to understand figurative language, **implied meanings**?
Is he able to understand **non-verbal cues**?
To what extent does he relate events in a **cohesive** (= forming a united whole) and **sequential** (= following in order of time or place) manner?
Does he make use of **repetitions**? Give examples.

Group 3: Try to assess **Christopher's flexibility of thought and imagination.**

This task should cover the following considerations:

What does the book reveal with regard to Christopher's **imagination**?
How easily can Christopher cope with **changes**?
What does **routine** mean in his life?
To what extent does he show **empathy** (= the ability to understand another person's feelings, experiences, situation, etc.)? Give examples.
What **fascinates** him?
How **sensitive** is he towards his environment?

Lösungsvorschlag zu *Copy 4:*

Christopher's **likes** and **dislikes**

☺	☹
dogs (cf. pp. 8, 10, cf. p. 8, l. 6)	lies (cf. p. 8, l. 4f., p. 27, ll. 1ff.)
wet and cold grass (cf. p. 8, llj. 22f.)	being shouted at (cf. p. 8, l. 12)
murder mystery novels (cf. p. 9, l. 12)	novels (cf. p. 9, ll. 3f., p. 28, ll. 3ff.)
the police and their uniforms (cf. p. 11, ll. 1f., l. 22)/the police cell (cf. p. 21, l. 14)	jokes (cf. p. 13, ll. 1–2, 9–14)
prime numbers (cf. pp. 17f.)	people (cf. p. 22, l. 1, p. 24, l. 13)
hospitals (cf. p. 32, ll. 6f.)	the colour brown (cf. p. 27, annotation)
red cars (cf. p. 33, ll. 1f.)	the colour yellow (cf. p. 33, ll. 4–9)
order (cf. p. 33, ll. 12–15)	being touched (cf. p. 12, l. 22, p. 24, ll. 9ff.)
being a detective (cf. p. 42, ll. 12f.)	

Group 1: **Christopher's social relations**

interaction with others	• does not defend himself, when Mrs Shears accuses him of having killed her dog (cf. p. 8, ll. 10–18) • starts his "groaning" when the policeman asks too many questions (cf. p. 12, ll. 5–20) • does not even show any response to the policeman's offensive way of dealing with him (cf. p. 14, ll. 5ff.) • cannot read people's minds (cf. p. 31, l. 23–p. 32, l. 2)
social rules	• hits the policeman after he touched him (cf. p. 12, ll. 21ff.), this again is interpreted as resistance to state authority • screams when a police officer wants to take his watch away because he needs to know the time (cf. p. 20, ll. 1ff.) • wants to write a "Get Well" card to his mother because it is a convention (cf. p. 32, ll. 26f.)
friends/ acquaintances/ people around him	**father:** runs his own small business (cf. p. 31, ll. 6f.); when Christopher is taken into custody (cf. p. 24), he obviously feels like hugging Christopher, but "spread[s] his fingers out in a fan" (p. 24, l. 10) to show Christopher that "he love[s him]" (p. 24, l. 14); advises his son to stay out of trouble, to mind his own business (cf. p. 29, ll. 8f., 12f., 16f., p. 30, l. 3) when it comes to the killing of Wellington (for good reasons, as in his attempt to make Christopher trust in him again, the father confesses "I killed Wellington" – p. 147, l. 19); uses vulgar language whenever he is upset (cf. p. 24, ll. 3f., p. 29, l. 21); hint at his relationship with Mrs Shears (cf. p. 38, ll. 4ff.) **mother:** Christopher remembers his mother, who "died two years ago" (p. 31, l. 1; in reality, she did not, but moved to London with her new lover) at the age of "only 38" (p. 37, l. 2) as a "small person who smelled nice" (p. 27, l. 4), someone who was "very active and rode a bicycle and ate food which was healthy" (p. 37, ll. 3f.); additionally, he mentions minor details (cf. p. 27, ll. 4–6); two chapters begin with sentences referring to his mother's death: indication how much this loss meant to him (cf. pp. 31, 36) despite his failure to tell us

friends/ acquaintances/ people around him	**Siobhan:** descriptive details (cf. p. 9, ll. 9f.); obviously his behaviour therapist, whom he met eight years before (cf. p. 6, l. 3; i.e. at the age of 7, most likely when his *Asperger's* was diagnosed for the first time), gives him many pieces of advice: cf. frequency of phrases such as "Siobhan said that I should" (p. 9, l. 2, cf. p. 9, ll. 17, 21, 23, p. 10, ll. 14f. etc.); helps him to understand facial expressions (cf. pp. 6–7, p. 22); helps him with spelling and grammar (cf. p. 35, ll. 23f.); has a considerable influence on his way of writing a *murder mystery novel* (cf. p. 9, ll. 17f.); takes him seriously: apologizes after she laughed at his way of coping with problems (cf. p. 7, ll. 4–13); knowing that he has a hard time understanding conventional orders, she tries to make her orders as precise as possible (cf. p. 39, l. 23–p. 40, l. 9) **Mr Jeavons:** the "psychologist at the school" (p. 33, l. 4, cf. p. 9, ll. 10f.), calls Christopher a "very logical person" (p. 33, l. 9f.) and "a very clever boy" (p. 33, l. 27) **Mrs Shears:** owner of Wellington, Christopher's neighbour with "bright pink" (p. 8, l. 9) toenails, whom he calls "our friend" (p. 5, l. 17); makes use of vulgar language (cf. p. 8, ll. 10f., 15f.) **Toby:** Christopher's pet = a rat (cf. p. 19, l. 12, p. 30, ll. 8ff.) **hints at his relatives** (cf. p. 20, ll. 6–10)
peer group/peer group pressure	**physically and mentally handicapped boys: Steve** (cf. p. 10, ll. 13–15)/**David** (cf. p. 32, ll. 15ff.)/**Francis** (cf. p. 34, ll. 24ff.) = hints that the kind of school which Christopher attends is a school for people with special needs • there is a hint that people outside of this circle try to ridicule Christopher (cf. p. 34, l. 24–p. 35, l. 2); however, Christopher is not put under pressure in any way by this (cf. p. 35, ll. 6–11).
importance of people's emotions	• contrast between Christopher's inability to see that Mrs Shears badly needs consolation (cf. p. 8) and the policewoman's corresponding reaction (cf. p. 11, ll. 7f.) • despite various clues (cf. p. 31, ll. 8–22, p. 32, ll. 3–13), Christopher entirely fails to notice that there may be serious reasons for his father not to look at him when speaking (it is only much later that the reader learns about the break-up of the parents' marriage, cf. p. 138, and that the ambiguous meaning of the father's former explanatory remarks becomes apparent, cf. p. 32, ll. 10, 12f.): Christopher only thinks it is "nice" (p. 32, l. 2) not to be looked at • on the other hand, he does take an interest in the people around him (cf. the story of Mrs Hardisty's death, p. 37)

Group 2: **Christopher's language and communication**

communication skills	• he hates being asked several questions in a row (cf. p. 12, ll. 5–11), too much information at a time (cf. p. 27, ll. 20ff.) • he has a hard time when questioned at the police station (cf. p. 25, ll. 3ff.); naturally, the policeman interprets this as a kind of refusal to cooperate with him • likewise, he totally disregards the father's and the policeman's attempts to help him out of his tricky situation (cf. p. 25, ll. 3f., 6f., 8f., p. 26, ll. 5–8), as his priority is the truth: white lies are not acceptable to him (cf. p. 25, ll. 23f.)

routine social interactions	• cannot stand being hugged by his parents; instead, he and his father touch by spreading their fingers out in a fan (cf. p. 24, ll. 9–14) • he cannot take orders (cf. p. 34, ll. 20f.), which he is aware of himself; nor can he understand simple orders appropriately (cf. p. 39, ll. 6f.); however, he is in a position to understand Siobhan's orders (cf. p. 39, ll. 23f.) • he also points out other people's habit of breaking rules, too (cf. p. 39, ll. 11–16), so in his eyes, he is not in any way exceptional • when informed about his mother's alleged death as a result of a heart attack, Christopher is mostly interested in the kind of heart attack and corresponding technical details, which seems a very inappropriate reaction for a son that has just been informed that his mother has just died; the father's reaction (cf. p. 37, ll. 6f.) is most likely the "normal" expected reaction to the loss of a beloved one
vocabulary	• his reflections on the Milky Way (cf. chapter 13) show that he knows very many related technical terms in the word field <u>astronomy</u>, such as "galaxy" (p. 15, l. 7), "lightyears" (p. 15, l. 2), "solar system" (p. 15, l. 3), "universe" (p. 15, l. 10), "starlight" (p. 15, l. 11), "billions and billions of stars" (p. 16, l. 8), "become extinct" (p. 16, l. 10) • similarly, he is in a position to use the appropriate technical terms in the word field <u>mathematics</u>, e.g. "cardinal numbers" (p. 17, l. 1), "prime numbers" (p. 17, l. 10), "positive whole numbers" (p. 17, l. 5), "multiples of" (p. 17, l. 7), "formula" (p. 17, l. 11) • after he learns that his mother has "died of a heart attack" (p. 36, l. 16), he shows that he knows technical terms from the word field <u>medicine/nutrition:</u> "high in fiber" (p. 37, l. 4), "low in saturated fat" (p. 37, l. 4), "aneurysm" (p. 37, l. 8), "embolism" (p. 37, l. 11), "blood clot" (p. 37, l. 11), "blood vessels" (p. 37, l. 12) • to sum up, in these areas of special interest, Christopher conveys the impression of a "little professor", a typical feature of many *Asperger's* children
sentence structure	• very often, Christopher's sentences are quite simple, mostly the linking words are "and" and "but" • he tends to repeat sentences (cf. p. 40, ll. 21 ff.)
implied meanings	• unable to understand the meaning of jokes (cf. p. 13, ll. 1 ff.) • unable to understand people "using metaphors" (p. 22, ll. 14–20, p. 23, ll. 6–11) • e.g. his clear distinction of metaphors and similes (cf. p. 25, annotation); Christopher himself uses and appreciates similes (cf. p. 25, ll. 1 f.) • comparison of life and prime numbers (cf. p. 18, ll. 7–10) • logical reasoning and weighing up of probabilities when it comes to evaluating clues related to the murder of Wellington (cf. p. 41, l. 3–p. 42, l. 5)
non-verbal cues	• unable to understand people's "talking without using any words" (p. 22, ll. 3f., cf. ll. 4ff.); to Christopher, this is too "complicated" (p. 22, l. 12) • able to describe people's behaviour very exactly without understanding the implications of it (cf. p. 26, ll. 9f.) • Christopher is aware of his problems when it comes to understanding non-verbal cues, which he describes with a simile (cf. p. 31, l. 23–p. 32, l. 1)

cohesive story telling	• typical of Christopher's style of storytelling are his mental leaps; he is easily diverted by topics that interest him all of a sudden, cf. breaks between chapters 5 ↔ 7, chapters 11 ↔ 13, chapters 13 ↔ 19, chapters 19 ↔ 23, whereas a clear relationship can be identified among chapters 2, 5, 11, 17, 23, 31, which all deal with the story proper, i. e. the murder and Christopher's confrontation with the police; chapters 3, 7, 13, 19, 29, 37 are deviations from this main story, although a connection can also be established here, namely his likes and dislikes • there are deviations from the chronological order, such as flashbacks (cf. chapter 43, pp. 31 f.) • Christopher is aware of this lack of cohesion (cf. p. 35, ll. 14 f.)
repetitions	• repeated use of "I said", "she said" throughout the book: rather than summing up the quintessence of a conversation, he retells everything in reported speech; unimportant details are not left out; all in all: long-winded, ponderous explanations • many sentences start with "And", "I"

Group 3: **Christopher's flexibility of thought and imagination**

imagination	• he cannot imagine things (cf. p. 9, ll. 18 ff.) or lie as it makes him feel scared (cf. p. 27, l. 7–p. 28, l. 2)
coping with changes	• he attaches great importance to "a nice order" (p. 33, ll. 12, 24, p. 34, l. 11); exception: being an astronaut (cf. p. 34, ll. 12–15) • he likes prime numbers (cf. p. 17, ll. 10 ff.): they have a certain pattern but cannot be grasped fully
routine	• being arrested by a policeman calms him down (cf. p. 16, ll. 1–4) because it is an expected reaction • red and yellow cars as a foreboding of good or bad luck is compared to other people's similar habits (cf. p. 33) • importance of time as a structuring device (cf. p. 20, l. 2) • shape of the police cell pleases him (cf. p. 20, ll. 14 f.)
empathy	• "I put the dog down on the lawn" (p. 8, l. 17): no pity, does not try to console Mrs. Shears • his way of showing empathy is different (cf. p. 30, ll. 15–24)
fascinated by	• "all the countries of the world, their capital cities and every prime number up to 7,057" (p. 6, ll. 1 f., p. 40, ll. 18–20) • "Apollo space missions" (p. 6, l. 9), the idea of being an astronaut himself one day (cf. p. 34, ll. 12–17), related topics such as the Milky Way and reflections on the end of the universe (cf. p. 16, ll. 1–13) • obsessed with figures (cf. p. 34, ll. 5–9), the possibility of studying mathematics or physics one day (cf. p. 35, ll. 7–10) • computer games (cf. p. 30, ll. 9–12) • the idea of building an "Airfix Sherman tank model" (p. 31, l. 5) • all in all: impression of the "little professor"

sensitivity towards environment	• he sees himself as somebody who is "being observant" (p. 34, l. 2), rather than clever (cf. p. 34, ll. 1 f.) • cf. his precise descriptions such as "for 4 minutes" (p. 8, l. 6), "2 meters" (p. 8, l. 17), "15 years and 3 months and 2 days" (p. 11, l. 16), "60 tiny circular holes" (p. 9, l. 11) – significantly, figures are not written out in words • description of the police (cf. p. 11, ll. 3–6): photographic view of things • cf. his detailed description of the content of his pockets (p. 19, ll. 7–16), i. e. he cannot tell important from unimportant (judged by common standards); precise and factual description of the police cell (cf. p. 20, ll. 14–20) • his sense of smell works very well (cf. p. 14, ll. 16f.) • all in all: great sensitivity to sensory stimuli (sounds, taste, touch, odours)

Word field *Asperger Syndrome*

alert	aufmerksam, aufgeweckt
anxiety	Angst
attention/attentive	Aufmerksamkeit/aufmerksam
to avoid social interaction	soziale Interaktion vermeiden
to behave differently from others	sich anders als andere benehmen
behaviour pattern/behaviour problems/children with behaviour problems/a checklist of behaviours with *Asperger Syndrome*	Verhaltensmuster/Verhaltensprobleme/Kinder mit Verhaltensproblemen/eine Checkliste für Verhaltensweisen bei *Asperger-Syndrom*
to be thought of as odd/unusual	für eigenartig /ungewöhnlich gehalten werden
bright child/smart kid	ein kluges Kind/ein schlaues Kind
consistent and structured routines	beständige und geregelte Routinen
to communicate with others	mit anderen kommunizieren
to curl up in a ball	sich zu einer Kugel aufrollen
deficiencies in social and communication skills	Defizite im sozialen und kommunikativen Bereich
depression	Depression
diagnosis/he was diagnosed with *Asperger/autism*	Diagnose/bei ihm wurde *Asperger/Autismus* festgestellt/diagnostiziert
to be different from contemporaries at school	anders als die Altersgenossen an der Schule sein
disorder/mental disorder	Funktionsstörung/Geistesstörung
gift/gifted	Talent, Gabe/talentiert, begabt
guidelines	Richtlinien
to handle social situations	soziale Situationen bewältigen
to have *Asperger Syndrome*	*Asperger-Syndrom* haben
to have an obsession with sth.	von etwas besessen sein
high intelligence	hohe Intelligenz
idiot savant (med., pej.)	geistig Zurückgebliebener, der auf einem bestimmten Gebiet außerordentliche Fähigkeiten besitzt
to ignore	nicht beachten, ignorieren
inattention/inattention problems/inattentive	Unaufmerksamkeit/Aufmerksamkeitsdefizite/unaufmerksam
indifference/indifferent	Gleichgültigkeit/gleichgültig
insane/mad	verrückt
lunatic/madman	irrer Mensch
mentally disabled	geistig behindert
mind	Geist, Verstand
nerd (infml)	Depp
routines/rules	Routinen/Regeln
smart Ale● (infml)	Schlauberger
specific pattern of behaviour	spezielle Verhaltensmuster
to understand facial expressions	Gesichtsausdrücke verstehen
talented	talentiert, begabt

2.3 Christopher and the police (chapters 11, 17, 23, 31)

Die herbeigerufene Polizei ist mit Christophers *Asperger*-typischem Verhalten zunehmend überfordert. Ihr mangelndes Verständnis ist dabei exemplarisch zu sehen: Die Sichtweise der Polizei verdeutlicht den Blickwinkel von sogenannten „normalen Menschen" auf einen „gestörten Menschen", wie Christopher es aus ihrer Sicht ist. Gemessen an herkömmlichen Rollenerwartungen kommt Christophers Reaktion den nicht geschulten Beamten wie aggressiver Widerstand gegen die Staatsgewalt durch einen Heranwachsenden vor und zieht entsprechende scharfe Gegenmaßnahmen nach sich.
Als vorbereitende Hausaufgabe für das *screenplay* sollte analysiert werden, wie sich das Verhalten der Polizisten gegenüber Christopher schrittweise wandelt, und danach den betreffenden Textpassagen entsprechende Wörter, die für den späteren Schreibauftrag benötigt werden können, zugeordnet werden.

Read chapters 11, 17, 23 and 31 closely and mark all those passages which reveal the police officers' feelings when dealing with Christopher. Additionally, look up words, which will help us to describe their emotions in each situation.

Zu erwarten ist folgendes Ergebnis:

passages	words to characterize the police officers' behaviour
p. 11, ll. 10f.	understanding, sympathetic
p. 11, l. 13	reaction as if Christopher had pulled his leg
p. 11, ll. 15, 17, 19, 27, p. 12, l. 2	normal interrogation
p. 11, l. 25, p. 12, l. 12	repeated questions, gradually starting to become impatient, irritated
p. 12, l. 21	puts Christopher (after one of his fits that must be inexplicable to the police officer) on his feet again, wants to carry on the normal interrogation
p. 14, ll. 1f.	outwardly: calm reaction after being hit by Christopher, takes Christopher into custody
p. 14, ll. 5–7	inwardly more upset, furious: insults Christopher by calling him a "little shit" and describing the whole incident as "monkey business"
p. 14, ll. 9–12	informs his colleagues using another derogatory remark/slang expression, namely "bugger" – style reflecting the world of criminals that they are usually confronted with
p. 20, ll. 1–4	at the police station, they want Christopher to take off his watch but do not go on using force when the boy starts screaming
p. 20, ll. 5f.	attempt to start a normal interrogation again
p. 20, ll. 14–20	helpless, tendency to overreact: Christopher is put into a cell as if he were a dangerous criminal

passages	words to characterize the police officers' behaviour
p. 25, l. 3–p. 26, l. 20	after a conversation with Christopher's father, the police inspector tries to be understanding and sympathetic towards Christopher, as he now understands the reasons for the boy's strange behaviour; while taking down Christopher's statement, he even seems to put the right words into his mouth; however, this goes unnoticed by Christopher
p. 26, ll. 9–20	eventually fed up with it all, frustrated that Christopher does not understand his concession; tries to be obliging, accommodating but at the same time is making clear that this is the very last chance

Eine Evaluation des Verhaltens der Polizisten ist folgendermaßen denkbar:

> What do you think of the police officers' way of treating Christopher? How do you think you would react if you were the policeman?

Hier wären folgende Reaktionen denkbar (auch als Hausaufgabe geeignet):

> On the one hand, it is absolutely unacceptable that the boy is called names by a representative of the state, someone who should under normal circumstances be a role model for behaviour, especially when dealing with young people who are in conflict with the law. On the other hand, however, the police are often confronted with resistance to state authority, even when having to do with juvenile delinquents. They cannot possibly know that Christopher is not simply one of those impertinent young people who intentionally try to give police officers a hard time by provoking them. Being hit by a 15-year-old boy for no reason at all, as it may have seemed to the policeman, makes him lose his patience. His form of behaviour seems only human.

Auf der Textgrundlage der Kapitel 11, 17, 23 und 31 sollen die Schülerinnen und Schüler anschließend in Gruppenarbeit ein *screenplay* erstellen. Die dabei zu beachtenden Vorgaben werden zunächst anhand des Arbeitsblattes *The opening act of a screenplay (Copy 6)* besprochen. Als Modell wird im Anschluss eine bereits ausgearbeitete Version, bezogen auf den Anfang des Buches/Kapitel 2, vorgelegt (*Copy 7*).
Die Aufgabe, die Vorgaben der entworfenen *screenplays* möglichst ideenreich und professionell umzusetzen und die Sequenzen vorzuführen, entweder live oder als gefilmte Version, sollten die Schülerinnen und Schüler als Hausaufgabe unter Verwendung entsprechender Requisiten (*gardening fork, cuddly toy, toy police car,* etc.) und Kulissen (*garden, bathroom,* etc.) vorbereiten.
Für die Präsentation der ausgearbeiteten Filmversionen und Kommentare müssen dann allerdings ca. 1 bis 2 Unterrichtsstunden eingeplant werden. Dies mag zeitaufwendig erscheinen. Man sollte aber den Spaßfaktor bedenken und auch, dass die Schüler bereits zu Hause freiwillig sehr viel Zeit investiert haben, bevor eine präsentable Filmversion entstanden ist.

Christopher and the police (chapters 11, 17, 23, 31) The opening act of a screenplay

The **screenwriter** of a film normally uses a **three-act structure**:

- **setup**: the **opening act** sets up the story and establishes the relationships between the characters (about 30 minutes)
- **confrontation**: in the second act, the conflict develops, the main character must overcome obstacles that keep him/her from achieving his/her goal and face crises (about 60 minutes)
- **resolution**: in the last act, the crises are overcome and the conflict is resolved (about 30 minutes)

When writing a screenplay, certain rules with regard to the **format** have to be considered:

- the screenplay is **typed in 12 point Courier** with **no bolding or italicizing**
- **slug lines** (= scene headings, scene captions) are typed in **capital letters** and answer three important questions: Are we inside (INT.) or outside (EXT.)? Where exactly are we? What time is it? (DAY/NIGHT/DUSK/EVENING/MORNING, etc.)
- **action lines (= descriptions** of the **settings** and the **action** that takes place) immediately follow the sluglines and are typed in lines of about **6 inches long**
- the **characters' names** are first introduced in the action line, typed in **capital letters**
- **wrylies** (= parentheticals): short instructions to the actor that come between the character's name and the dialogue, descriptions of how a character says something and what he/she should do when speaking, put in parentheses
- **dialogue** is **centred** on the page, the lines are about **3 inches (i. e. 7.6 cm) long**

Now finally, get started …

- re-read all the relevant passages which have to be adapted for film
- make notes on the following aspects (**setting**: Where do the scenes take place? When do they take place?/**atmosphere**: What information is given in the text? What props are needed?/**characters**: Who is mentioned in each scene? How do they behave, move? What gestures do they make? What facial expression have they got? How can their feelings be visualized?/**action**: What happens in each scene?/**direct speech**: Who says what? How should it be said?)
- present and discuss your ideas in groups of 4 people (4 actors-to-be),
- decide who should be in charge of the individual chapters mentioned above and start writing individually (so that everybody has a clearly defined task): don't forget **"MOVIES MOVE"** (i. e. show more than tell)
- when all have finished, take turns in proofreading, suggest changes if necessary
- most importantly: **be prepared to perform the scenes in class** (rehearsals after school) – alternatively, the scenes can be filmed at home and shown to your classmates in one of the following lessons.

Example of proper formatting (chapter 2)

```
EXT. STREET, LAWN WITH GATE IN FRONT OF HOUSE - NIGHT

15-year-old CHRISTOPHER has just found dead dog WELLINGTON,
pinned down by a garden fork, goes through gate, kneels be-
side dog, pulls fork out, hugs dog for quite a long time.

                        MRS SHEARS
                       (infuriated)
                   What in fuck's name have
                     you done to my dog?

CHRISTOPHER does not answer, looks scared.

                        MRS SHEARS
                   (yelling, hysterical)
                 Let go of the dog. Let go of
                 the fucking dog for Christ's
                           sake.

CHRISTOPHER puts dog on lawn, moves 2 metres back, very
scared. MRS SHEARS bends down to dog. CHRISTOPHER watch-
es her, not knowing what to do.

                        MRS SHEARS
                  (screaming blue murder)

CHRISTOPHER puts hands over ears, eyes closed, curls up
in a ball, forehead pressed onto grass.

                       CHRISTOPHER
                     (groaning sound)

MRS SHEARS, in a panic, runs to the house, shortly after-
wards, a police siren can be heard blaring, MRS SHEARS
comes out again, a POLICEWOMAN and a POLICEMAN get out of
the police car.

                       POLICEWOMAN
                     (to MRS SHEARS)
                 Mrs Shears, let's go inside.
                   Superintendent Clark will
                      take care of this.

POLICEWOMAN puts arm round MRS SHEARS.
```

Component 3

Solving two mysteries

In diesem dritten *Component,* der sich auf die Kapitel 59–167 bezieht, werden sich die Schülerinnen und Schüler mit Besonderheiten des Genres *murder mystery novel,* der klassischen Detektivgeschichte in Anlehnung an Arthur Conan Doyle, beschäftigen und anschließend überprüfen, inwieweit der Roman Konventionen dieser Gattung aufgreift. Darüber hinaus führt Christophers Suche nach dem Mörder Wellingtons zu einem zweiten Mysterium, das es zu lösen gilt, nämlich der Frage, warum es noch anderthalb Jahre nach dem vermeintlichen Tod der Mutter Briefe an ihren Sohn gibt, die von ihr verfasst und an ihn gesandt wurden, ihm aber offenbar vom Vater vorenthalten wurden. Die Lösung dieses zweiten Rätsels wiederum führt zur Lösung der eigentlichen Detektivaufgabe. Durch die Person des Vaters sind beide Handlungsstränge miteinander verwoben: Christopher muss erfahren, dass der Vater die Geschichte vom Tod seiner Frau erfunden hat, um dem Sohn die aus seiner Sicht wohl unangenehmere Wahrheit von ehelicher Untreue und mangelnder Fürsorgepflicht für das gemeinsame Kind zu ersparen. In seiner Verzweiflung über die Trennung von seiner Frau und deren Hinwendung zum Nachbarn einerseits und die als zu gering eingeschätzte Zuneigung der Nachbarin zu ihm selbst andererseits hat der Vater schließlich den Hund dieser Nachbarin getötet. Die Wirkung dieser Erkenntnisse auf Christopher bleibt nicht aus. Vom Vater hinsichtlich des Schicksals der Mutter belogen worden zu sein, führt bei Christopher zu starker Übelkeit und temporärem Bewusstseinsverlust. Dass der Vater darüber hinaus der Mörder des Hundes ist, löst schlimmste Befürchtungen in ihm aus, sodass für ihn als einzige Möglichkeit das Verlassen der vertrauten Umgebung und die Flucht vor diesem Menschen infrage kommen.

3.1 Christopher's investigation into the murder of Wellington

Als visueller Impuls dienen eine kopierte Abbildung von Sherlock Holmes (siehe *Copy 10)* sowie folgende auf Folie geschriebene Zitate aus dem Roman (Gedankenblasen):

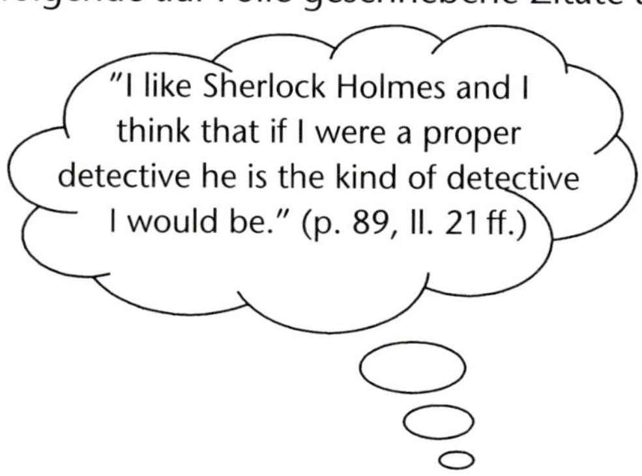

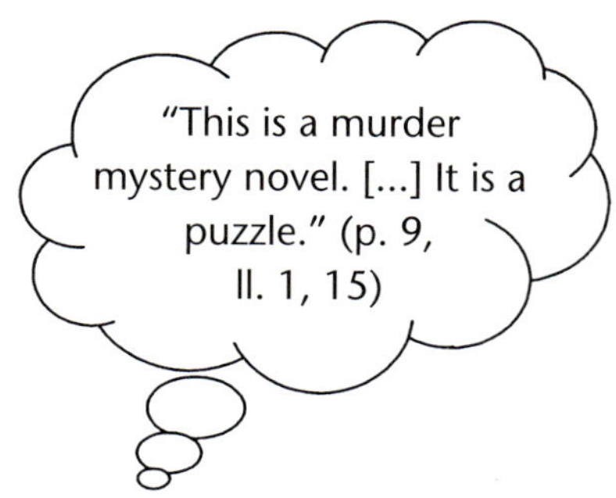

Für den Fall, dass den Schülern Arthur Conan Doyles Detektiv kein Begriff sein sollte, ist doch davon auszugehen, dass aufgrund der Vielzahl von Filmen zum Thema typische Elemente dieses Genres in einem *brainstorming* unkommentiert an der Tafel gesammelt werden können. Folgende Fragen können ergänzend eingesetzt werden:

Do you know any of Sherlock Holmes's personal attributes and character traits?
Explain his working methods as a detective.

Denkbar ist folgendes Tafelbild (alternativ: Folie, Lehrervortrag oder vorbereiteter Schülerkurzvortrag):

Sherlock Holmes

- a fictional detective of the late 19th and early 20th centuries
- apartment in Baker Street/friend: Dr Watson
- devised by Scottish author and physician Sir Arthur Conan Doyle
- **personal attributes:** a deerstalker hat (= *Mütze mit Ohrenklappen)* (cf. *Curious Incident,* p. 91, ll. 4–5, in contrast to this)
  an oversized hooded duster (= *langer Kapuzenmantel)*
  a pair of spats (= *Gamaschen)*
  oversized magnifying glass/curved pipe
- **character traits:** absolutely honest/analytical mind/logical/rational/autonomous/superior/almost superhuman/slightly aristocratic manners/slightly snobbish/eccentric
- **working methods:** close **observation**: he uses his five senses, i. e. he sees, hears, smells, feels, tastes everything

  investigation: he talks to witnesses and suspects, gathers evidence, shadows people
  eventually solves the riddle, the intellectual crossword puzzle, the inexplicable by **deduction**: normally conclusion reached by reasoning from general laws to a particular case, here: collecting pieces of information, combining them, eliminating the impossible, drawing conclusions until finally a problem is solved

  reconstruction: putting the pieces of a puzzle together

  intuition: he sometimes understands situations immediately without any reasoning

Im Anschluss können typische Elemente von *detective stories* zusammengetragen werden:

What examples of detective stories, both in literature or film, do you know?
What elements and characters are typical of a murder mystery novel?
Sometimes, the solution is deliberately delayed. How is this achieved?
Do you like stories where the perpetrator has to be found out by the detective?
What effect does it have on the reader's role if the story starts out with the murder and the identity of the murderer is revealed to the reader only?
What are the advantages of inverted chronology (murder – reasons for murder)?

Im Unterrichtsgespräch kann ein Tafelbild *Basic elements of detective fiction* (alternativ: Präsentation einer Folie als Zusammenfassung/*Copy 8)* erstellt werden.
Anschließend werden die gesammelten Kriterien mithilfe eines Arbeitsblattes auf Haddons Roman übertragen (*Copy 9*).

Die drei Fragen am Ende dieses Arbeitsblattes *Copy 9* eignen sich als Anregung für ein Essay. Da es sich dabei um einen umfangreicheren Schreibauftrag handelt, könnte dies als Hausaufgabe gestellt werden.

Folgende Antworten zu den *while-reading tasks (Copy 9)* sind denkbar:

working methods	• Christopher observes closely (cf. p. 41, ll. 4–6)/he tries hard to investigate without being noticed himself (cf. p. 40, l. 28–p. 42, l. 8)/draws conclusions (cf. p. 41, ll. 19–20, p. 42, ll. 3–5)/wants to find things out (cf. p. 42, l. 12)/he works on his own (cf. p. 46, ll. 5f.)/in his eyes, the work of a detective requires courage (cf. p. 47, l. 13, p. 72, ll. 1–4, p. 74, ll. 11–14)/he carefully plans his strategy (cf. p. 47, ll. 15ff.)/he is ready to defend himself with a knife (cf. p. 48, l. 1, p. 150, ll. 5f.)/he explains his "Chain of Reasoning" (p. 54, l. 6, cf. ll. 5–22), a form of the method of deduction/wants to avoid a *"Leap to the Wrong Conclusions"* (p. 121, l. 21)/he insists that people answer his questions and even puts them under pressure (cf. p. 73, l. 24–p. 73, l. 29)/he collects evidence for or against someone and possibly excludes former suspects who prove to be innocent from his investigations (cf. p. 74, ll. 12ff.)/ability to fully concentrate on sth just like his role model Sherlock Holmes (cf. p. 90, ll. 1–22)
suspects	• Mrs Shears?, counter-arguments (cf. p. 41, ll. 23–25)/Mr Shears = "prime suspect" (p. 54, l. 22, cf. p. 55, ll. 12–22, cf. p. 63, ll. 5–7)
witnesses	• the boy turns to neighbours for help, e.g. Mrs Shears (cf. p. 40), the Thompsons (cf. p. 48, l. 5–p. 49, l. 8), the black family (cf. p. 49, l. 10–p. 50, l. 9), Mr Wise and his mother (cf. p. 50, ll. 16–25), Mrs Alexander (cf. p. 51, l. 3–p. 54, l. 4)
alibis	• Mr Thompson's brother presents an alibi, which Christopher does not call into question (cf. p. 49, ll. 6–8)
clues	• the gardening fork in Mrs Shears's shed = murder weapon (cf. p. 41, ll. 12–22)/he gives examples of clues from Conan Doyle's detective story *The Hound of The Baskervilles* (cf. p. 88, l. 11–p. 89, l. 4)/however, although the father repeatedly and firmly warns his son not to interfere in other people's business (cf. p. 39, ll. 1f.) and gets extremely furious when he finds out that his son has disregarded his instruction (cf. p. 63, l. 12–p. 63, l. 29, p. 99, l. 16–p. 102, l. 8), Christopher totally fails to notice the real reasons why/similarly, the black lady's early hints at the culprit's identity (cf. p. 49, ll. 19f., p. 50, l. 6) are not considered by Christopher, either • even the fact that Mrs Shears "sometimes [...] stayed overnight at our house" (p. 55, l. 3) does not make him think further/moreover, he is unable to add Mrs Alexander's repeated hints at the connection between his parents' relationship and the murder of Wellington (cf. p. 72, ll. 29f., p. 73, ll. 1ff., 16, 18, 22f., p. 73, ll. 30f., p. 76, ll. 3f.) to the puzzle
red herrings	• Christopher's definition of a red herring (cf. p. 41, ll. 20–22)/examples of red herrings from Conan Doyle's story (cf. p. 89, l. 5–p. 89, l. 22) • in connection with the hidden book, Christopher uses and explains the term "Double Bluff" (p. 114, l. 4)

criminal	• conviction that the murderer and his victim are often very close (cf. p. 54, ll. 16ff., cf. p. 67, ll. 19f.)/at this point Christopher, ironically enough, is not aware how close he is to the solution of the crime (foreshadowing device, anticipation)
solution	• Christopher's image of his father before the father's confessions: "he always tells me the truth, which means that he loves me" (p. 107, l. 21) • the solution to the second mystery: "Mother had not had a heart attack. Mother had not died. Mother had been alive all the time. And Father had lied about this." (p. 138, ll. 11ff.), an idea which Christopher can hardly stand; his world is turned upside down: "I felt giddy. It was like the room was swinging from side to side, as if it was at the top of a really tall building and the building was swinging backward and forward in a strong wind. [...] I rolled onto the bed and curled up in a ball. My stomach hurt. I don't know what happened then because there is a gap in my memory like a bit of the tape had been erased. [...] And I had been sick because there was sick all over the bed and on my hands and arms and face." (p. 138, l. 16–p. 139, l. 3)/Christopher seems almost numb, paralysed after this revelation; he cannot respond to his father's attempts to help him (cf. p. 139, ll. 22f., p. 141, ll. 3, 14ff., p. 167, ll. 8, 11, 14, p. 146, l. 24) • the father's confession (cf. p. 147, l. 19) seems like a joke at first (cf. p. 147, ll. 20f.), then, he is scared (cf. p. 149, l. 6); his father's desperate attempts at explaining his deed (cf. p. 148) do not seem to count: "Father had murdered Wellington. That meant he could murder me. [...] I wondered if he [...] was waiting to come in and kill me. [...] I could hear the blood in my ears and my heart going really fast and a pain like someone had blown up a really big balloon inside my chest.[...] [M]y legs were shaking." (p. 149, ll. 22f., p. 150, ll. 4f., 15ff., p. 151, ll. 1f.)

Hier ein Lösungsvorschlag zu den drei abschließenden Fragen *(Copy 9):*

With regard to the question of whether Christopher is a good detective or not, it can be said that on the surface and in theory, he definitely is. Just like his role model Sherlock Holmes, he ambitiously tries to track down the offender and to apply all the relevant techniques that he learned about in Arthur Conan Doyle's fiction.
At the same time though, he is not in a position to read between the lines or consider people's emotions appropriately: A whole set of clues is missed due to this limited perception.
Moreover, walking around with his Swiss Army Knife just in case he might be attacked by the murderer seems a bit naïve. He does not seem to be aware that the first to fall victim to this weapon could very well be he himself.
To sum up, one might say that, theoretically, Christopher is well aware of all the conventions of the detective story and that several aspects of Christopher's personality might make him an ideal detective. In practice, though, he must necessarily fail.
So, despite the fact that his thorough investigation drove the culprit into a corner and made him confess it all, which is by common standards the highlight of every detective's effort, Christopher cannot enjoy this

success at all. The supposed triumph turns out to be a personal disaster for him. Not only did his father lie to him about his mother's fate, so that he can never trust in him again, but the father is, in the eyes of his son, an evil, ruthless person, who might even become a danger for his own son.

However, this revelation, very sad as it might seem at first glance, is the trigger for Christopher's escape from the familiar surroundings, which poses a big challenge for him. The boy is taken on a coming-of-age adventure by his investigation. Whereas the detective story has come to an end, the story proper, namely Christopher's story, has only just begun. The two layers of the action are interwoven: Childlike blind trust is replaced by the extreme disappointment of an adolescent, a development which will, all the same, give Christopher the chance to become independent in the end. In the long run, cutting the cord is necessary to become an adult, to overcome his helplessness as revealed at the end of the episode with his father: "Then I wondered what I would do next." (p. 151, l. 26) Considering the difficulties that Christopher has with regard to new people and places, it will not be easy for him to find his way in the world alone, without any mentor at his side. Now that he knows that his mother is still alive, he will probably want to contact her. He might turn to Siobhan for help, although she will most likely be the person that his father will also contact first of all. Additionally, he does not have any friends or neighbours who might support him. What is more, he has never left Swindon before.

So the question is, will Christopher have the courage to be responsible for himself or not? And if so, will he be able to make it in an alien world?

Man kann nun über den weiteren Fortgang des Romans spekulieren oder/und den Auftrag erteilen, ein *word field detective stories* zu erstellen (alternativ: *Copy 10*).

Durch the Simulation einer Gerichtsverhandlung *(simulating a court-case)* sollen the Schüler das freie Sprechen, Debattieren und Argumentieren einüben.

Zur Vorbereitung der Gerichtsverhandlung sollte den Schülern entsprechendes Vokabular bekannt sein. Die *role-cards (Copy 11)* geben Anregungen zu den beteiligten Charakteren und sollten noch weiter ausgearbeitet werden. Die Vorbereitung auf die Rollen und das entsprechende Wortfeld kann als Hausaufgabe gestellt werden. Für die eigentliche Verhandlung sollten 1–2 Unterrichtsstunden eingeplant werden.

Imagine Mrs Shears did what is called "pressing charges" (p. 251, l. 13), i.e. making the police arrest Mr Boone for killing Wellington.

What to do:[1]

1. Prepare the following seating arrangements:

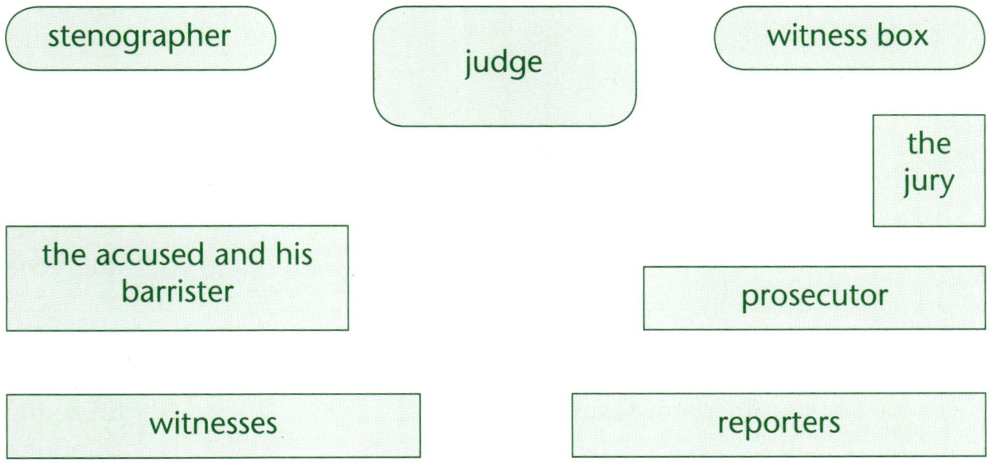

2. At the beginning, the judge presents the case. He/She points out that Mr Boone is accused of the murder of Wellington.
3. The prosecutor and the barrister give their point of view in opening statements. Mr Boone may give his point of view.
4. Witnesses (Christopher, Mr Wise, Mrs Alexander, the policeman, the "drug"-people from next door, the woman from house No. 44, cf. *Curious Incident,* pp. 46–50) are interrogated. Other witnesses may be Mr Shears, Siobhan, Rhodri or Mrs Boone who can report on Mr Boone's character or behaviour.
5. The jury (= a group of members of the public who listen to the facts of a case in a court and decide whether or not sb is guilty of a crime) may ask questions.
6. The prosecutor and the barrister sum up their opinion in front of the judge and jury and plead guilty or not guilty.
7. The jury withdraws for about five minutes and makes a decision.
8. The judge gives his/her judgement and passes the sentence or releases the accused.
9. The reporters interview the people involved. The newspaper reporter for the tabloid press writes an article. The TV reporters present the case in a report on the news on TV (which can be video-taped and shown to the class in the next lesson).
10. The stenographer types the record of the case and hands it in in the next lesson.

[1] Nach einer Idee von Beyer-Kessling, Viola et al.: *Die Fundgrube für den handlungsorientierten Englisch-Unterricht.* (Berlin 1998), S. 77–80.

Basic elements of detective fiction

Exposition	Developing action	Conclusion
Crime →	→ Detection →	→ Solution
• the case, intricately planned • mystery/puzzle/ confusion	• working methods • reasoning power • aim: to reveal parts of the mystery step by step	• explanation/insight • hunting down the perpetrator • triumph of the detective/victory of good over bad
Victim • usually human being • arouses people's attention, evokes pity	**Detective** • amateur, mostly superior to the police • protector of society/protagonist	**Criminal** • enemy of society, broke the law/ antagonist • often the least suspected character
	Suspects/Prime Suspect • those most suspected of having committed the crime are mostly least likely to be the criminals **Alibi** • evidence that proves that a person was in another place at the time of a crime and so could not have committed it	
	Witnesses • support the detective (or the criminal)	
	Clues • hints that help to find answers to the difficulties the detective is confronted with	
	Red Herrings • wrong tracks, devices in the story that are meant to lead both the characters in the story and the reader astray, draw the attention away from the real criminal	
	Reader's Position • follows the detective's line of thought, sides with him/her	

Christopher's investigation into the murder of Wellington
While-reading tasks (chapters 59–167)

Try to find out to what extent Christopher sticks to the conventions of crime fiction by…
• identifying Christopher's **working methods** as a detective 
• listing the **suspects** that he keeps an eye on 
• finding out whether he questions **witnesses** and relies on **alibis** 
• identifying **clues** 
• and **red herrings** 
• judging whether the **criminal** identified by Christopher bears resemblance to typical criminals in crime fiction 
• evaluating whether the **solution** is in line with typical detective stories (i. e. triumph of the detective), and deciding whether similarities of differences predominate 

- How convincing is Christopher as a detective?
- Why does the story not end right after his solution to the crime?
- What might the rest of the story be dedicated to?

Word field *detective stories*

The detective …

arrogant/honest/implacable, relentless/omniscient/self-absorbed	hochnäsig/ehrlich/unnachgiebig/allwissend/mit sich selbst beschäftigt
detective/amateur detective/investigator/sleuth	Detektiv
mastermind	Superhirn
to be motivated by curiosity	von Neugierde getrieben sein
logician	logisch denkender Mensch, Logiker

His/her investigating methods …

the case	der Fall
clues/hints/to discover a clue	Spuren/Hinweise/eine Spur entdecken
detailed investigation into a mysterious murder/to investigate sth	detaillierte Untersuchung eines mysteriösen Mordes/etwas untersuchen
detection	Aufdeckung von Verbrechen
to deduce sth/deduction/to draw a conclusion	schlussfolgern/Schlussfolgerung/eine Schlussfolgerung ziehen
to dig deeper	der Sache auf den Grund gehen
to discard several possibilities	mehrere Möglichkeiten ausschließen
to expose/to unmask sb as sth	jmd. als ... entlarven
to follow up on a clue/to follow sb secretly	eine Spur aufnehmen/jmd. heimlich verfolgen
the gradual revelation of the truth	die allmähliche Enthüllung der Wahrheit
investigation into sth	Untersuchung von etwas
to know more than the (foolish) police	mehr als die (dümmliche) Polizei wissen
to put oneself in sb's place	sich in jmd. hineinversetzen
to ransack sth	etwas durchwühlen
to search a room thoroughly	einen Raum gründlich durchsuchen
to shadow sb/to trail sb/to tail sb	jmd. beschatten
to snoop about	herumspionieren
to solve the case by keen observation/by logical reasoning	den Fall durch scharfe Beobachtung lösen/durch logisches Denken
to take up the trace of sb	die Fährte von jmd. aufnehmen
to track a criminal down	einen Kriminellen ausfindig machen

The criminal …

an alibi	ein Alibi
to be wrongfully accused	falsch beschuldigt werden
to commit a crime/the commission of a crime	ein Verbrechen begehen/das Begehen eines Verbrechens
criminal/offender/culprit/perpetrator	Krimineller/Straftäter/der Schuldige/Täter

motive	Motiv
to murder sb/murderer/murder	jmd. ermorden/Mörder/Mord
to pull the wool over sb's eyes/to take sb in	jmd. hinters Licht führen
to be suspected of having done sth/to fall under suspicion of -ing/suspicion/to seem suspicious to sb	im Verdacht stehen, etw. getan zu haben/Verdächtigung/jmd. verdächtig vorkommen

The detective story ...

detective story/whodunit	Kriminalgeschichte
to create tension/suspense	Spannung erzeugen
the given facts	gegebene Tatsachen
exposition/climax/turning point/denouement, solution	Einleitung/Höhepunkt/Wendepunkt/Auflösung
improbable possibility	unwahrscheinliche Lösung
to look over the detective's shoulder	dem Detektiv über the Schulter schauen
a mystery/a puzzle	ein Rätsel/ein Puzzle
the mystery revolves around murder	... geht es um Mord
red herring/false clue	falsche Spur
to reveal the most unlikely person as murderer	die unwahrscheinlichste Person als Mörder entlarven
solution to the puzzle	die Lösung des Puzzles
tension	Spannung
watertight plotting	hieb- und stichfeste Handlung

further words:

§§ The trial – the murder of Wellington (role-cards) §§

The people involved	Their tasks/attitudes
judge	You organize the proceedings and give a short outline of the case.
stenographer	You keep the minutes of what is happening in court.
jury (4 people)	You will have to decide if Mr Boone is guilty or not guilty.
barrister	You try to prove Mr Boone's innocence.
public prosecutor	You try to prove that Mr Boone is guilty of the murder of Wellington.
The accused **Mr Boone**	You say that it was only self-defence because Wellington had rabies and wanted to attack you.
Christopher	You report how you found the dog and what happened afterwards. You talk about your father's confession.
Mrs Shears	You strongly dislike Mr Boone because he didn't want you to move into his house. Also, there was that night when you had that really bad fight …
Mrs Boone	You present your former husband's behaviour during your marriage. You have to decide whether he is capable of such a deed. (look for clues in her letter, cf. pp. 129–138)
member of *Pro Animal*	You are a member of a group to protect animals. You are angry about Mr Boone and say he tortured Wellington to death.
Mrs Alexander (neighbour)	You are a nice old lady with a dog and your dog was friends with Wellington. You are very angry about the murder of the poor dog.
the "drug people" (neighbours)	You think you remember the incident because there was a nightmarish devil with a fork fighting with a black werewolf …
the black woman (neighbour)	You never liked Wellington and you were afraid that he could bite your two children because Mrs Shears never put her dog on the lead.
Mr Wise (neighbour)	You were awake that night because your old mother was keeping you busy. You heard a quarrel outside and weird noises. You went to the window and saw …?
the policeman	You found Christopher lying on the ground next to the stabbed dog. You like Mr Boone and think that he is taking the blame himself to protect his son.
Mr Shears	You don't like Mr Boone because your lover (Mrs Boone) told you that he never cared about her. And there was also the fight you once had with him because …?
Rhodri	You like Mr Boone, who is your boss and your friend. Moreover, you know that a conviction would be very negative for Mr Boone's business.
Siobhan	You know the family quite well and are afraid that Christopher is suffering as a result of the situation. Nevertheless, you think Mr Boone is very patient and reliable.
newspaper reporter(s)	You are from the Swindon tabloid press and want to make a big story out of it because usually nothing interesting happens in Swindon.
TV reporter(s)	You are interested in the trial. You are eager to get a good story.

3.2 The second mystery – The truth about Mrs Boone

Durch die Briefe von Christophers Mutter wird die Perspektive des Romans verändert. Hinsichtlich der Familienkonstellation konnte man bisher davon ausgehen, dass bedingt durch einen schweren Schicksalsschlag Christophers Vater die große Verantwortung für einen heranwachsenden, leicht behinderten Sohn allein übernehmen musste. Aus Rücksicht auf den Jungen schien es verständlich, ihn nicht zur Beerdigung mitzunehmen.

Plötzlich zeigen nun die Briefe, dass Mrs Boone in Wirklichkeit Mann und Sohn verlassen hat, um mit einem Mann, dem ehemaligen Nachbarn Mr Shears, ein neues Leben in London zu beginnen. Unverständnis tritt an die Stelle von Bedauern für diese Frau.

Um die Schüler anzuregen, Fragen an Christophers Mutter zu stellen, könnte man ein Rollenspiel zum Thema *Being a woman today: wife? mother? lover?* in Kleingruppen von ca. fünf Schülern vorbereiten lassen, und zwar angelehnt an im Fernsehen weit verbreitete *chat shows (Copy 12).*

Alternativ kann man folgenden Impuls an die Tafel schreiben, der zu Kommentaren und Fragen anregen soll:

> Mother leaves her only child,
> a handicapped teenage boy,
> to live in London with her new lover.

Zu erwarten sind dabei folgende Gedanken, die sich an der Tafel sammeln lassen:

What were the **reasons** why you went away?
How did/do you get along with **Christopher**?
  Didn't you have the feeling that you were responsible for him?
  Didn't you realize that he wasn't getting your letters?
How did your **marriage** develop?
  Did you have the feeling that your husband would be able to cope with single parenthood?
To what extent did your relationship with **Roger** contribute to your decision?
  Didn't you have any **feelings of remorse**?

What is your **present attitude** towards leaving husband and child?
  Would you still take this decision? Why? Why not?

With regard to the **future,** have you thought about any **alternatives** yet?

What do the letters reveal?

Eine detaillierte Lektüre der Briefe beantwortet diese oder ähnliche Fragen wie folgt: (Antworten in der 3. Pers. Sg.)

reasons	
Christopher	• looking at old photos makes Mrs Boone sad, although she likes happy Christmas memories (cf. p. 129, l. 16, p. 129, ll. 17f.) → however, really good times were exceptional • in one of the letters, Mrs Boone describes a typical fit of her son's during her Christmas shopping at a department store called Bentall's (cf. p. 131, l. 8–p. 132, l. 3) → you can imagine very well that shopping with Christopher was no fun at all, to outsiders he must have seemed a real pain in the neck

	• in the course of an argument over food with his mother, Christopher's behaviour resulted in his mother's broken toes (cf. p. 133, l. 13, ll. 24–25), so that Mr Boone had to take care of their son (cf. p. 133, ll. 25ff.) • it is important to Mrs Boone to let her son know the whole story (cf. p. 132, l. 22–p. 133, l. 6); she "never meant to hurt [him]" (p. 134, l. 25) and so she writes one letter a week, sometimes even two letters (cf. p. 135, ll. 18f.), moreover, there is a picture of her son on her desk (cf. p. 136, l. 7); she also sends him presents (cf. p. 137 ll. 5–9)
husband/ marriage	• Mrs Boone explains why she left Christopher with his father; she presents her husband as a parent who is by nature much more capable of dealing with a difficult child (cf. p. 132, ll. 4ff.) • this impression is enforced when you look at Mrs Boone's reaction after the episode at Bentall's (cf. p. 132, ll. 4–13) → Mrs Boone describes her husband as someone who could take care of the boy like a mother and as a husband who tried to calm her down; at the same time, she conveys the impression that their married life suffered a lot in the long run: there was physical and verbal aggression • the argument over Christopher's eating habits emphasizes the parents' different ways of dealing with Christopher's peculiarities: the father is again described as someone who did not put the blame for his wife's broken toe on Christopher because he knew that their son could not help it (cf. p. 133, ll. 19–23) • The father's and mother's ways of dealing with Christopher after this argument were opposed (cf. p. 133, ll. 27–28) → as a consequence, she felt excluded and useless (cf. p. 133, l. 27, p. 134, ll. 1f., p. 134, l. 3) • in the end, they decided to stop talking altogether, which was the end of a proper relationship (cf. p. 132, ll. 13–16); the next step in the deterioration of their marriage was loneliness (cf. p. 132, ll. 16f.) • the married couple was caught up in a **vicious circle** of **problems with their common child – stress – arguments – aggression – end of communication – loneliness – openness to a new relationship – sharing common interests – falling in love** • Mr Boone prevented his wife from seeing their son and explaining to him why she left (cf. p. 134, ll. 13–24)
Roger	• Mrs Boone adopted a typically female role (cf. p. 130, ll. 11f.) • the reason why Mrs Boone turned to Mr Shears in the first place was her need to talk to someone after she had almost stopped communicating with her husband (see above "husband/marriage") and to be understood (cf. p. 132, ll. 14ff.) • two obstacles were in the way of Mrs Boone starting a relationship with Mr Shears, namely his marriage, which existed only theoretically, and her son (cf. p. 132, ll. 26ff.) • his decision to work in London put pressure on her (cf. p. 134, ll. 8–12)
personal contribution **feelings of remorse**	• she is aware of her personal shortcomings (cf. p. 131, l. 1) • referring to the Christmas shopping at Brentall's, Mrs Boone repeatedly describes herself as someone who could not put up with the challenge of Christopher's handicap very well (cf. p. 131, l. 16–p. 132, l. 3) → on the verge of a breakdown • she is aware that hitting her husband in one of these arguments "was wrong" (p. 132, l. 9), although she knows that it only happened because she was so upset (cf. p. 132, l. 10) • the final argument between Christopher and his mother about a normal parent-child topic, namely the son's eating habits (cf. p. 133,

(cont.)	ll. 7–20), made Mrs Boone lose her temper (cf. p. 133, ll. 16f.) → reaction seems very exaggerated, but it reveals that Christopher had already shattered his mother's nerves • after this argument, he started thinking that father and son would be better off without her (cf. p. 134, ll. 5f.), although she did not easily consent to Roger's renewed invitation to join him (cf. p. 134, ll. 8–10, p. 134, ll. 10–22)
present attitude	• no explicit comment, but from all the observations listed above, it seems justified to say that Christopher's mother misses her son a lot (one and even two letters a week)
future	• "I used to have dreams that everything would get better." (p. 135, l. 1)
alternatives	→ very vague • would love to fly kites with her son or watch the planes flying into Heathrow (cf. p. 136, ll. 25ff.) → indulges in nostalgic idylls, disregarding that Christopher is not a little child anymore

Eine Antwort auf die Briefe bietet sich als schriftliche Hausaufgabe an, und zwar aus dem Blickwinkel des Vaters unter Verwendung der Hinweise der Mutter und aus Textstellen, die das Rollenverständnis des Vaters erhellen. Ein Arbeitsblatt zum Verfassen eines informellen Briefes *(Copy 13)*, verbunden mit dem Verweis auf entsprechende Textstellen, erleichtert diese Aufgabe. Hier ein Modellbrief:

Swindon, 20th Oct. 1997

Hi Judy,

This morning on the radio they happened to play the old Kenny Rogers song "You picked a fine time to leave me, Lucille, four hungry children and a crop in the field" and automatically I was reminded of the situation I'm in at present ... You wouldn't believe what it means to raise Christopher alone without anybody to help, because you've never been in a situation like this and never will be. You simply decided to clear off instead ...

Very often, when I have to do heating maintenance and boiler repair with Rhodri, as life is not cheap these days and someone has to earn the money, I hardly see the boy at all. He is left to himself many times a day, although he mostly keeps himself busy. He's not stupid, you know he isn't. Then it's me who has to fix him something to eat and worn-out as I am, I have to do the laundry after work, and take him to the doctor and settle arguments at school and many other things. I'm there when he wakes up at night. I calm him down when he's upset. Who else would do this for him now, if not me? In the neighbourhood, I don't dare to ask anybody to look after him when I'm not there. There are idiots like Mr Thompson's strange brother walking around with T-shirts saying "BEER Helping ugly people have sex for 2,000 years". And the people next door are always on drugs. That's the way it is. But I'm telling you no secret. Nobody to turn to ... And you know yourself that Chris is not always easy to get along with.

I still remember when you came home after you had been Christmas shopping with him and had the feeling that he had made a fool of

himself in the shop with all the people staring at you and him. He never did anything to you on purpose, though. The doctors told us many, many times that this simply is the way he is. We'd better put up with it. We wouldn't easily be able to change him. But you wouldn't listen, ever. Why couldn't you accept him the way he is? After all, he's your child as well. You're his mother, a really fine mother, I must say. To me, your behaviour is something I cannot and will never accept. Then, how could you let yourself in with this bloke? How stupid you are. Do you think he will take care of you when you really need someone, when you are old and ugly? Forget it. I know quite well what he's after, from the moment I first met him, he has always been like that. Didn't you think of your son when you went to bed with this horny bastard? Like a slut!
Meanwhile, you have been gone for about 18 months and now I really wish you would simply leave us alone – FOR GOOD. We have had to do without you. We can manage alone. Mind your own business. Do whatever you like but stop writing to Christopher. He's not talking about you anyway. He doesn't even seem to miss you at all.

Ed

Being a woman today: wife? mother? lover? *(role-play)*

The situation

… Just imagine a popular **chat show** on TV, a programme which is made up of informal interviews. Next to the chat show host, who asks the questions, there are telephone calls from members of the public included, which is called **phone-in**.

The topic is "Being a woman today – wife? mother? lover?"

Women from different backgrounds will be interviewed about the way they see themselves. This evening, Mrs Boone, a woman who decided to change her small community life entirely by leaving her husband and a 15-year-old handicapped son in order to start a new life in the capital, is the guest.

Your tasks

In small groups (of about 5 pupils) prepare a role play on this topic related to the information in *The Curious Incident of the Dog in the Night-Time*. The characters are

The chat show host, Mr or Mrs Dolittle
- you need to introduce Mrs Boone and briefly present her decision
- above all, you are interested in a cracking story with regard to viewer ratings (= *Einschaltquoten*)
- you want to ask her provocative questions

Christopher's mother, Mrs Boone
- first of all, you tell the story of your former life in Swindon, your marriage and parenthood and secondly, you describe your life as it is now
- then be ready to answer embarrassing questions (therefore, you must be absolutely familiar with the content of "your" letters)

Members of the public
… namely
Mrs Jones (a devoted mother of 6 children)
Mr Miller (whose wife divorced him for a new lover)
Ms Anybody (a Londoner) … or other people of your choice
- you want to find out more about Mrs Boone's decision
- you ask her as many questions as possible
- you tell Mrs Boone if her arguments are not convincing

Mr Boone's letter to his ex-wife

The situation: Imagine Mr Boone has already received more than 40 letters addressed to Christopher. Finally, he decides to write his former wife a letter himself …
In case you need any ideas, you may want to use the frame below and consider some of the following passages from Mrs Boone's letters, e.g.

- p. 131, ll. 1ff./p. 132, ll. 4–16/p. 132, ll. 16–23/p. 133, l. 25–p. 134, l. 3/p. 134, ll. 13–22

and/or some of the passages where Mr Boone's way of speaking and behaving, his situation in general is revealed, e.g.

- p. 24, ll. 1f./p. 30, ll. 1–6/p. 43, ll. 6–16

Use extra paper if you run out of space.

Swindon, 20th Oct. 1997

Hello Judy,

This morning on the radio they happened to play this old Kenny Rogers song "You picked a fine time to leave me, Lucille, four hungry children and a crop in the field" and automatically I was reminded of the situation I'm in at present ...
You wouldn't believe ____________________

____

____

____

____

I still remember when ____________________

____

____

____

____

To me, your behaviour is ____________________

____

____

____

____

Meanwhile, you have been gone for about 18 months and now I really wish ____________________

____

____

____

____

Ed

Component 4

Christopher's journey

Component 4 liegen die Kapitel 167–233 zugrunde. Mit Kapitel 167 erreicht Christophers Geschichte zugleich ihren Höhepunkt *(climax)* und einen Wendepunkt *(turning-point)* in seinem Leben. Zunächst bietet es sich an, den strukturellen Aufbau narrativer Texte mit den Schülern zu erarbeiten und anschließend die Fachbegriffe auf Christophers Geschichte bis einschließlich Kapitel 167 anwenden zu lassen (*Copy 14*).
Die Lehrperson aktiviert eventuelles Vorwissen und ergänzt die Fachtermini an der Tafel. Zur Festigung sollen die Schülerinnen und Schüler mithilfe von *Copy 14* Fachbegriffe und deren Bedeutung zuordnen und den strukturellen Aufbau einer Geschichte grafisch darstellen.
In lernschwachen Gruppen können die Fachbegriffe und die entsprechenden Erklärungen vorgegeben werden. Die Schüler werden aufgefordert, die Begriffe und die entsprechenden Erklärungen in Partnerarbeit zuzuordnen und anschließend die Fachbegriffe in das Diagramm von *Copy 14* einzufügen und auf die bereits gelesenen Kapitel von *The Curious Incident of the Dog in the Night-Time* anwenden. Das Diagramm sollte gegebenenfalls im Verlauf der Lektüre weiter vervollständigt werden.
Abschließend können die Schüler ihren Vorschlag in das Diagramm einzeichnen, erläutern und mögliche andere Kurvenverläufe diskutieren. Die Ergebnissicherung kann abschließend am Overhead-Projektor erfolgen.

Lösung zu *Copy 14* (Zuordnungsaufgabe):
1d/2c/3f/4a/5b/6e

Is the model graph on the worksheet valid for every narrative text? Does Haddon's story correspond to or deviate from this model? Draw your own graph and explain your choice.

Mögliche Antwort:

It is only a basic story structure, but there can be other solutions. With regard to Haddon's novel, for example, it is also possible to illustrate the degree of suspense in the story-line with ups and downs (vgl. Lösungsvorschlag: green curve). The degree of suspense sometimes rises or falls from chapter to chapter and can be shown in the form of a curve. For example, at the beginning the level of suspense is quite high when Christopher describes the scene of Wellington lying dead on the lawn with a garden fork stuck in the body. In chapter 3, the level of suspense may be considered lower as we only get to know a few facts about Christopher without much action in between.

Literary terms and the structure of a story

Cut out the cards. ✂ -
Match the *literary terms* with the appropriate definition.

Literary terms[1]	Definition
1) **exposition**	a) increase of suspense and the intensification of the conflict
2) **falling action**	b) the final outcome when the conflict is resolved
3) **climax**	c) development marked by a reduction in suspense
4) **rising action**	d) element at the very beginning, which includes at least some of the following: introduction of the main character, theme, setting, atmosphere or the tone
5) **denouement**	e) moment marking a change in the conflict
6) **turning point**	f) the moment when the conflict is most intense

Write the *literary terms* from above into the diagram below.
Try to apply these terms to Mark Haddon's novel up to chapter 167.
Give text evidence and support your decision by facts.
Draw a graph.

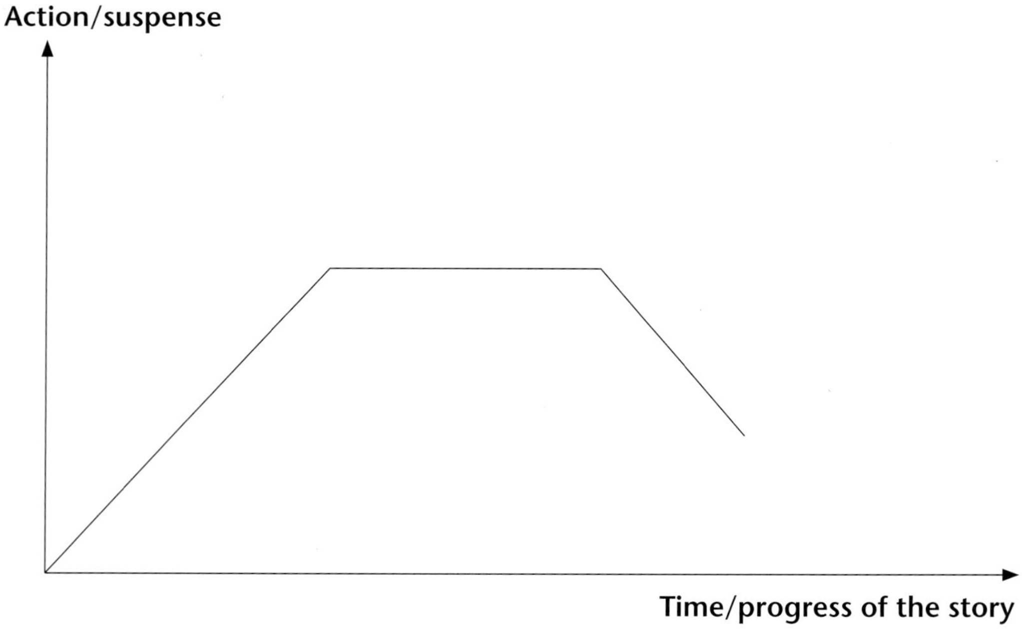

[1] Cf. *Student's Glossary of Literary Terms*, Cornelsen 2004

Lösungsvorschlag zu *Copy 14* (Graph zu *Curious Incident*):

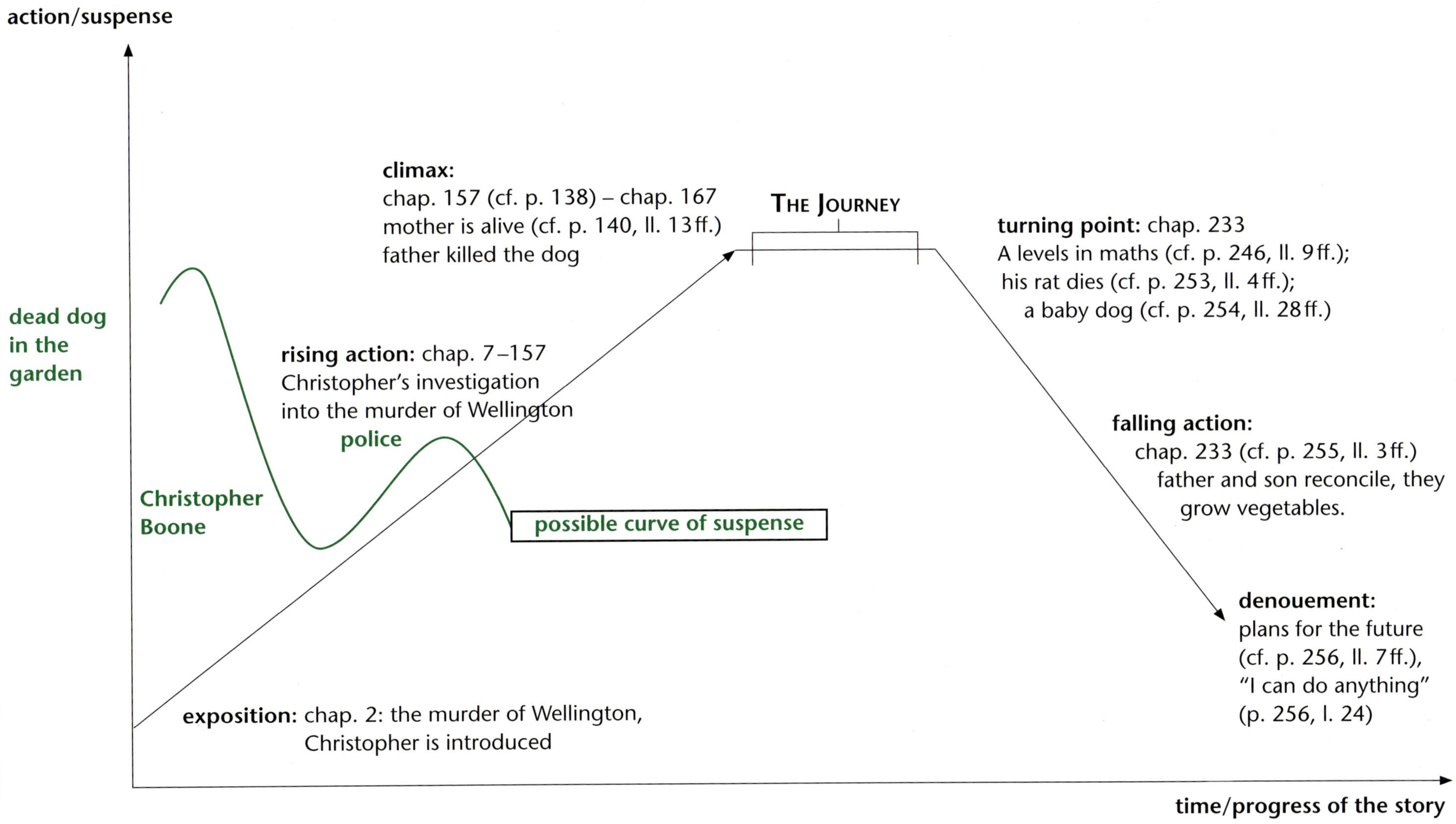

4.1 Getting to London

Dieser Abschnitt bezieht sich auf die Kapitel 179–233; hier soll Christophers äußere *(literal/external)* und innere *(spiritual/internal)* Reise erarbeitet werden.
Die folgenden Kapitel weisen typische Merkmale einer Initiationsgeschichte *(story of initiation)*[1] auf.
Als Einstieg in das Thema Initiationsgeschichte ist *Copy 15* als Folienvorlage vorgesehen. Anhand der Abbildung und des Impulses in der Gedankenblase soll im Unterrichtsgespräch zusammengetragen werden, welche Prozesse und Lebenserfahrungen ein Kind oder Jugendlicher durchlaufen muss, ehe er erwachsen ist.

Where is the difference between the adult and the child that you can see in the picture?
What experience does the father have in contrast to the child?

Die Schülerinnen und Schüler werden neben dem körperlichen Entwicklungsprozess, den das Kind durchlaufen muss, eventuell auch auf die eigenen Erfahrungen, Konflikte und Probleme zu sprechen kommen, die ein Jugendlicher vor allem in der Pubertät bewältigen muss.
Anschließend sollen die Schülerinnen und Schüler die Definition der *story of initiation* auf Mark Haddons Roman anwenden. Das kann begleitend zur Lektüre geschehen oder abschließend zur Einordnung des Romans in das Genre der *story of initiation.* Hierzu besteht die Möglichkeit, den Schülerinnen und Schülern das *Word field story of initiation* auszuhändigen *(Copy 16),* beziehungsweise ein solches von Schülerinnen und Schülern erstellen zu lassen.

Story of initiation

The youthful protagonist of a story of initiation gains his experiences during a **journey** which consists of the three phases of **exit**, **transition** and **(re-)entrance** and leads the traveller from **innocence** to **experience**. In the course of the journey, he experiences different, mostly unexpected, bewildering, and disillusioning **confrontations** with a world hitherto unknown, which finally lead him to some decisive **insight** or **recognition** which changes his life.

(Peter Freese)

journey	both literal and spiritual
confrontation	conflicts
insight	shock, disillusionment, discovery of the disparity between appearance and reality

Die Schülerinnen und Schüler sollen erkennen, dass die Offenbarungen des Vaters Christopher zum Verlassen *(exit)* seiner Lebenswelt veranlassen. Ihm wird durch die schonungslose Konfrontation mit der Realität seine Lebenswelt *(innocence)* genommen. Der Austritt aus seiner Lebenswelt ist für Christopher unausweichlich, da er im Gegensatz zum Leser die Verhaltensweise seines Vaters nicht nachvollziehen kann. Sein Vater wird für ihn zur Bedrohung, was ihn zwingt, nach Alternativen im Leben zu suchen.

[1] Vgl. Freese, Peter: „Über die Schwierigkeiten des Erwachsenwerdens: Amerikanische *stories of initiation* von Nathaniel Hawthorne bis Joyce Carol Oates", in: ders., *The American Short Story I; Initiation,* Paderborn, 1984.

At the beginning of initiation stories, there is usually an exit.
Read pages 158–164 of the novel closely and identify passages which indicate that Christopher leaves his old world behind.

text passages	their meaning
"And then I realized that there was nothing I could do which felt safe." (p. 158, ll. 1f.)	without any orientation at first
"And then I thought how I could never be an astronaut [...] And it made me sad to think that I could never become an astronaut." (p. 159, ll. 9f., p. 159, ll. 18f.)	the father's confession triggers off Christopher's flight and exit from his former life/his world and everything meaningful to him breaks apart
"I had to go to London to live with mother." (p. 158, ll. 9f.)	the only alternative to his present life seems to be his mother's apartment in London
"And then I thought that I had to be like Sherlock Holmes and I had to *detach my mind at will to a remarkable degree* [...] And then I *Formulated a Plan."* (p. 159, ll. 20 ff.)	he finds help in Arthur Conan Doyle's detective stories, so that he can develop strategies to get to London
"I tried to open the kitchen door but it was locked. So I picked up a brick that was lying on the ground and I smashed it through the window and the glass shattered everywhere. Then I put my arm through the broken glass and I opened the door from the inside." (p. 162, l. 9–p. 162, l. 12)	this passage has a symbolic meaning as it reflects the boy's current situation: his former life is not accessible to him any more/ the father's confession has destroyed his trust just as a brick destroys a window. His life is broken like a window pane in front of him, opening the door is not altogether without any risk, which again bears resemblance to his life at present: he will have to open doors by himself and be in danger; he might easily hurt himself

Um diese *imagery* zu verdeutlichen, kann der Lehrer eine Skizze, eventuell unter Vorgabe der eingerahmten Wörter, an die Tafel zeichnen, um diese zentrale Textstelle (p. 162, l. 9–p. 162, l. 12) abschließend von den Schülerinnen und Schülern zusammenfassen zu lassen:

Mögliches Tafelbild:

Christopher leaving home

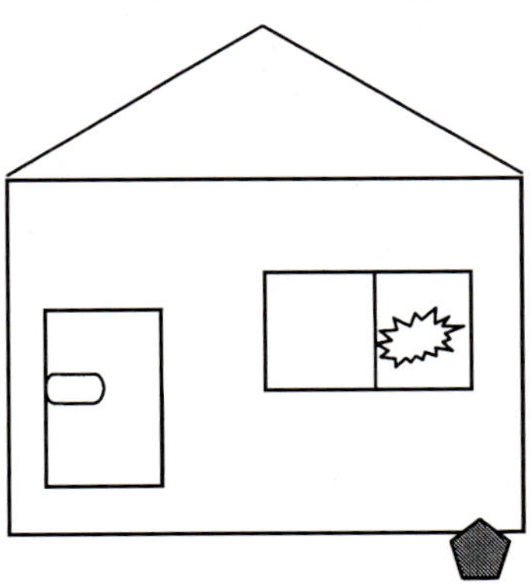

house → safe, protected shelter of his former life

window → Christopher can look at the world outside, but is protected inside (broken pane → no protection)

door → Christopher has to face the outside world and leave his shelter

brick → father's confession, loss of protection

Als Vorbereitung auf den nächsten Arbeitsschritt kann die von Christopher erstellte Skizze von *Great Britain* (cf. p. 198) als Folienvorlage verwendet werden.

Have a look at the picture. What do you think is shown?
What purpose does this unusual presentation of Great Britain serve?

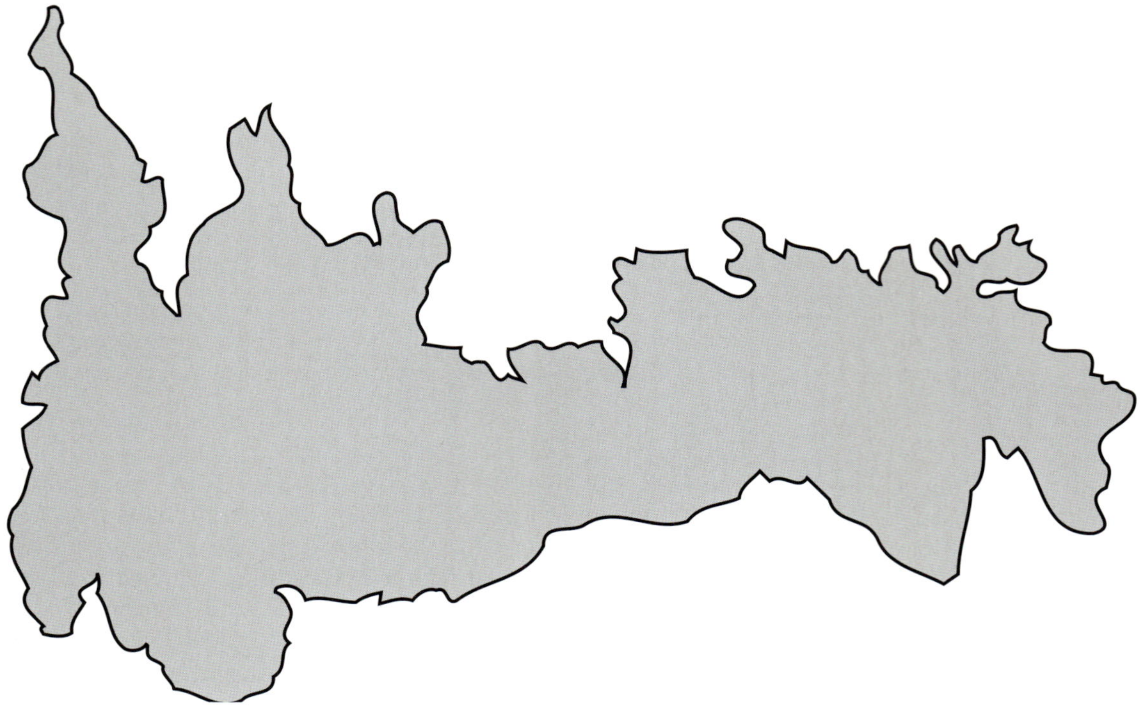

Die Abbildung zeigt die Umrisse von Großbritannien. Die Karte ist entgegen der herkömmlichen geographischen Darstellungsweise nach rechts gekippt dargestellt. Dadurch, dass die Schülerinnen und Schüler die Darstellung ohne die markierte Route von Swindon nach London präsentiert bekommen, können sie im Unterrichtsgespräch einen Eindruck davon gewinnen, welche Herausforderung diese vergleichsweise unkomplizierte Reise für einen Menschen wie Christopher bedeuten mag. Erneut wird deutlich, dass sich seine Wahrnehmungen erheblich von denen anderer Menschen unterscheiden.
Falls gewünscht, kann der Lehrer die Route Swindon – London zu einem späteren Zeitpunkt einzeichnen oder durch ein Folien-*Overlay* ergänzen.
Fakultativ kann Christophers tatsächliche Reise *(external journey)* anhand von Kartenmaterial von Swindon und London (U-Bahnkarte) von Schülern präsentiert werden. Anders als im Buch angegeben, gibt es in Swindon zwar keine *Randolph Street,* lediglich eine *Randolph Close.* Christophers Strategie, sich dem Bahnhof von Swindon in immer kleiner werdenden Kreisen zu nähern, kann man auf diese Art in etwa nachvollziehen (vgl. S. 167, Z. 1–6, S. 167, Z. 7–11). Die *Chapter Road* existiert tatsächlich in London und ist über die *Bakerloo Line/Willesden Junction (Willesden Green)* zu erreichen.

Zur übersichtlichen Darstellung von Christophers Reise empfiehlt es sich, eine Wandzeitung *(wall display)* zu entwerfen, auf der sowohl Christophers genauer Reiseverlauf *(external journey)* als auch seine innere Entwicklung *(internal journey)* während der Reise dokumentiert wird. Die Schüler können den Verlauf der Reise fortlaufend in ihr Heft übertragen.

As you already know, the story of initiation consists of the basic elements of exit, transition, re-entrance. How can this development best be illustrated in the form of a graphical presentation?

Die kreisförmige Basisstruktur von Christophers Reise sollte vom Lehrer vorgegeben werden, wenn die Anregung dazu nicht von Schülerseite kommt. Das Verlassen seiner Alltagssituation bedeutet für den Protagonisten eine Konfrontation mit Problemen, für die er eine Lösung finden muss. Gleichzeitig entwickelt er sich durch diese Konfliktsituationen weiter, sodass es ihm nach seinem Wiedereintritt (Swindon) möglich ist, seine Lebenssituation wiederherzustellen.
Es empfiehlt sich, die Basisstruktur für die folgende Arbeit in drei Elemente zu unterteilen, und zwar zunächst bezogen auf seinen äußeren Reiseverlauf und anschließend auch auf seine innere Entwicklung:

Part 1: The trip to London
Part 2: Finding shelter in his mother's apartment
Part 3: Future perspectives

Basisstruktur: ***wall display***

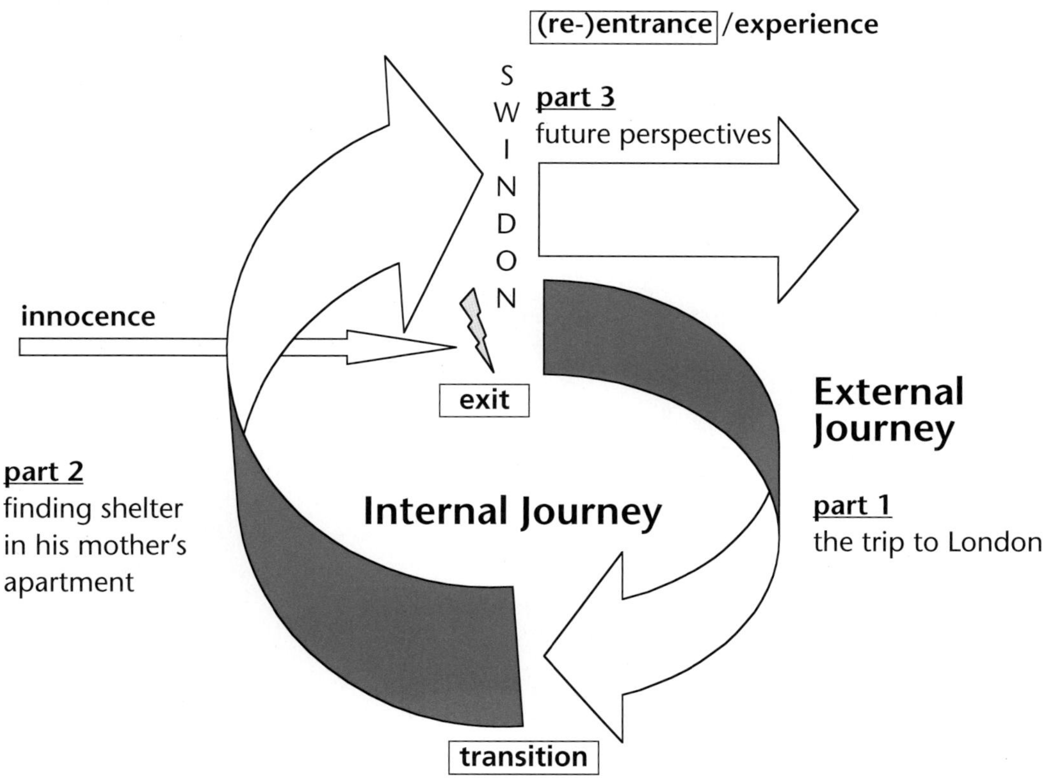

Der nächste inhaltliche Schwerpunkt liegt auf der Art und Weise, wie Christopher die anstehende Reise meistert:
Immer dann, wenn er sich von einer Situation überfordert fühlt, stellt sich Christopher an verschiedenen Stationen seiner Reise eine rote Linie *(guide-line)* am Boden vor, die ihm hilft, Schwierigkeiten zu bewältigen und seinen Weg fortzusetzen.
Entsprechende Textstellen können auf Folie vergrößert und präsentiert werden. Ergänzend kann ein realer roter Faden eingesetzt werden.
Nicht nur für Christopher als Jugendlicher mit *Asperger-Syndrom* ist es wichtig, den sprichwörtlichen „roten Faden" im Leben nicht zu verlieren, sondern dies gilt für jeden Menschen, besonders aber in der oft schwierigen Phase des Selbstfindungsprozesses in der Jugend.
Auf seiner Reise *(journey)* erhält Christopher Hilfe und Unterstützung von verschiedenen Personen *(guides),* die ihm bei Schwierigkeiten zur Seite stehen. Ein solcher Begleiter ist z. B. der Polizist, der ihm am Bahnhof in Swindon hilft, ein Ticket zu kaufen und in den richtigen Zug zu steigen. Hierzu zählen auch andere Reisende, die ihm Auskünfte geben, Hilfe anbieten oder ihn davor bewahren, von der U-Bahn überfahren zu werden.

What difficulties do you expect when you go on an unknown journey?
Why is it particularly difficult for a person like Christopher to go on such a journey?
What could he do to cope with this situation?
Have a look at the following quotations from the novel:

"And I pictured in my head a big red line across the floor which started at my feet and went through the tunnel and I started walking along the red line [...]." (p. 184, ll. 18–20)

"So I stood up and imagined that there was a big red line on the ground which ran parallel to the train to the gate at the far end and I walked along it [...]." (p. 200, ll. 18–20)

"Then I imagined a red line on the floor and I walked over to the wall where there was a poster which was a list of places to go and it was alphabetical [...]." (p. 205, ll. 12–14)

What does Christopher do to overcome the difficulties?
What do you associate with "red line"?
Read the passages on Christopher's journey closely (beginning/leaving home: "I went out", p. 163, l. 16/end/arrival at mother's place: "So I decided to wait", p. 224, l. 14).
Make notes on the following aspects

- confrontations/challenges during his journey
- Christopher's strategies to cope with the challenges/guides, helpers

How might the passages you found be added to the *wall display?*

Wall display/part 1: The trip to London

SWINDON

EXTERNAL JOURNEY

lady with a baby helps him to find the way to the train station (cf. p. 165, l. 8–p. 165, l. 30)

he makes a plan to move in a spiral (cf. p. 167, l. 1–p. 167, l. 11)

finds his way to the station (cf. p. 167, l. 11)

policeman helps him to get on the train (cf. p. 178, l. 12–p. 181, l. 10)

policeman wants to take him home (cf. p. 189, l. 20–p. 194, l. 15)

lady at the information desk in London (cf. p. 203, l. 11–p. 204, l. 5)

imitation of other passengers' behaviour (cf. p. 205, ll. 8–11)

man with a green raincoat saves his life (cf. p. 215, l. 14–p. 216, l. 12)

lady with a guitar case offers help (cf. p. 216, l. 15–p. 217, l. 10)

a man in a shop sells him a street map of London (cf. p. 220, l. 15–p. 221, l. 17)

innocence

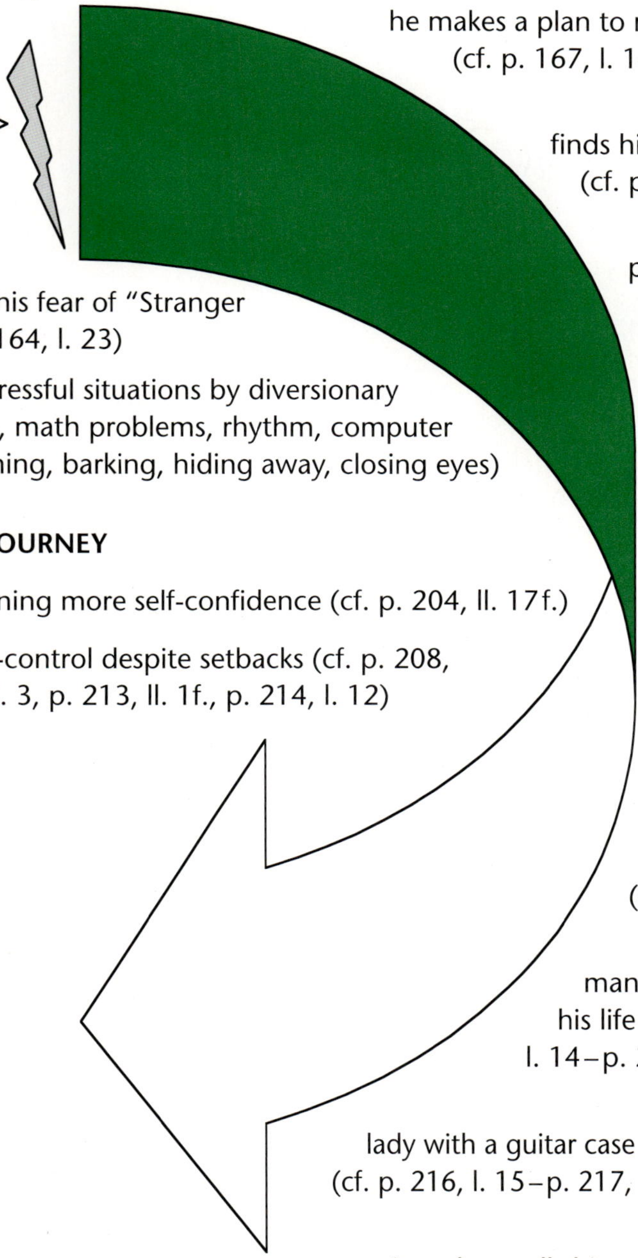

tries to fight his fear of "Stranger Danger" (p. 164, l. 23)

overcomes stressful situations by diversionary tactics (maps, math problems, rhythm, computer games, groaning, barking, hiding away, closing eyes)

INTERNAL JOURNEY

gradually gaining more self-confidence (cf. p. 204, ll. 17f.)

fights for self-control despite setbacks (cf. p. 208, l. 4–p. 210, l. 3, p. 213, ll. 1f., p. 214, l. 12)

Father and son

Word field *stories of initiation*

age/phases of life

birth/birthday/born	Geburt/Geburtstag/geboren
baby	Baby (d.h. bis ca. 2 Jahre)
toddler	Kind, das gerade laufen lernt
infant	Kleinkind (Kindergartenalter)
child – children/childhood/kid (informal)	Kind – Kinder/Kindheit/Kind
schoolboy/schoolgirl/schoolchild	Schuljunge/Schulmädchen/Schulkind
puberty	Pubertät
youth/young	Jugend, Jugendlicher/jung
teenager	Teenager (d. h. zw. 13 und 19 Jahren)
adolescent/adolescence	Heranwachsender/Jugendzeit
young adult/adulthood	junger Erwachsener/Erwachsenenalter
marriage/to get married (to)	Ehe/jmd. heiraten
aged/old	betagt/alt
grown-up/to grow up	Erwachsener/erwachsen werden
to be of age/to be under age	volljährig sein/minderjährig sein
old age	Alter
death/dead	Tod/tot

character development

innocence/the innocence of childhood	Unschuld, Naivität/die Unschuld der Kindheit
the movement from childhood to adulthood	die Entwicklung vom Kindes- zum Erwachsenenalter
to pass from childhood into maturity	von der Kindheit zum Erwachsensein gelangen
crisis – crises	Krise – Krisen
adolescent behaviour	pubertäres Verhalten
maturity/knowledge/experience/the experience of adulthood	Reife, Erwachsensein/Wissen/Erfahrung/die Erfahrung des Erwachsenseins
to gain experiences	Erfahrungen sammeln
an insight which changes sb's life	eine Einsicht, die jds. Leben verändert
recognition	Erkenntnis, Einsicht
the recognition of one's identity and role in the world	das Bewusstsein der eigenen Identität und Rolle in der Welt
disillusioning/disillusionment	frustrierend/Frust, Enttäuschung, Ernüchterung

literary terms

story of initiation	Initiationserzählung
coming of age novel/apprenticeship novel	Bildungsroman
youthful protagonist/youthful character	jugendliche(r) Held(in)
a transitional process	ein Übergangsprozess
rites of passage	Übergangsriten
mentor	Mentor, d.h. jmd., der einem zur Seite steht

4.2 Digressions from the journey: Astronomy and religion

Während seiner Reise ergänzt Christopher sein Buch um Kapitel, in denen er von seinem eigentlichen Reiseverlauf abweicht *(digressions)*. Diese gedanklichen „Abstecher" von Christophers Reiseroute werden hier getrennt behandelt, sind aber ein wichtiger Teil seiner Reise. Sie erlauben uns in Ergänzung zu *Component 2* einen erneuten Einblick in Christophers Denkweise. Die Kapitel, die sich mit Christophers Lösung mathematischer Probleme beschäftigen, können als Referatsthemen von Schülern erarbeitet werden (siehe Konzeption des Unterrichtsmodells, S. 23).

Christophers Abstecher in die Themengebiete Astronomie und Religion werden an dieser Stelle aufgegriffen.

In Kapitel 173 und 179 wird geschildert, wie Christopher von seinem Versteck hinter dem Gartenhäuschen das Sternbild „Orion" betrachtet, weil er sich für Astronomie interessiert und Astronaut werden möchte.

Da für ihn lediglich Fakten zählen, ist für ihn die Vorstellung, im Sternbild „Orion" die Figur eines Jägers zu sehen, nicht nachvollziehbar, sondern eine Verfälschung der Realität. Hier kann ein Referat zum Thema „Sternbilder" vorbereitet werden.

In Kapitel 199 erörtert Christopher den Konflikt zwischen Religion und Wissenschaft in Bezug auf Evolution. Aufgrund der beiden recht unterschiedlichen Anschauungen kann man hier fächerübergreifend bzw. fächerverbindend (Religion/Biologie) arbeiten. Dies erleichtert den Schülern den Zugang zu den beiden unterschiedlichen Denkrichtungen. Vorab ist alternativ ein Referat zu Darwin und Evolutionstheorie denkbar.

Bereits in Kapitel 61 (vgl. S. 32–34) wurde deutlich, dass Christopher die Vorstellung eines göttlichen Himmels nicht akzeptiert. Als Einstieg dient folgende Situation:

Imagine the following situation. You are the grandmother/grandfather of a little child, whose mother, your daughter-in-law, is in hospital. She has very little chance of recovering again. Soon after, you learn that she has died after surgery. You must tell your grandchild. What can you say to console your grandchild?

Hier werden vermutlich herkömmliche Denkmuster (Himmel, lieber Gott, etc.) genannt werden. Vor diesem Hintergrund wird Kapitel 61 (vgl. S. 43–45) anschließend laut gelesen und danach eine kurze Stillarbeitsphase mit folgender Aufgabenstellung erteilt:

What different ideas concerning dying, God and heaven does Christopher present in this chapter?

passages	their meaning
"Mrs Forbes said at school that when Mother died she had gone to heaven." (p. 43, ll. 1f.)	conventional approach
"But when mother died, she didn't go to heaven because heaven doesn't exist." (p. 43, ll. 7f.)	inadequate explanation in the eyes of Christopher
"I said that there wasn't anything outside the universe and there wasn't another kind of place altogether." (p. 43, ll. 16f.)	he clearly rejects the idea of heaven as a place where God resides
"I think people believe in heaven because they don't like the idea of dying because they want to carry on living..." (p. 44, ll. 3–4)	to him the conventional approach was invented by people because they could not cope with the idea of being gone for good

passages	their meaning
"The Reverend Peters said, "Well, when I say that heaven is outside the universe it's really just a manner of speaking. I suppose what it really means is that they are with God." (p. 44, ll. 7f.)	theologians use heaven as an image to illustrate the idea of a being above human beings
"And I replied, 'But where is God?'" (p. 44, l. 10)	to Christopher the idea of God is equally unacceptable
"What actually happens when you die is that your brain stops working and your body rots […] (p. 44, ll. 13f.)	scientific approach favoured by the boy
"And all his [i.e. Christopher's rabbit's] molecules were broken down into other molecules and they went into the earth and were eaten by worms and went into the plants and if we go and dig in the same place in 10 years there will be nothing except his skeleton left." (p. 44, ll. 15–19)	circle of life from a biologist's point of view
"But mother was cremated." (p. 44, l. 25, cf. p. 44, l. 27–p. 45, l. 3)	he even sees his mother's death rationally

In Kapitel 199 greift Christopher die konträren Vorstellungen von Religion und Wissenschaft wieder auf. Er erklärt, warum er nicht an die Erschaffung der Welt durch Gott glaubt, sondern die Evolutionstheorie nach Darwin für wahrscheinlicher hält.

In chapter 199, Christopher deals with the question of how universe and life came into existence. He compares religious ideas to scientific ideas and draws a conclusion.
→ List the different ideas.
→ What point of view does Christopher favour? Explain why.

religious ideas	scientific ideas (by Darwin)
"People believe in God because the world is very complicated […]." (p. 196, ll. 1f.)	There is life on earth because of an accident (cf. p. 196, l. 12) and replication, mutation and heritability. (p. 196, ll. 15–20)
It is very unlikely that anything as complicated as the human eye came into existence by chance. (cf. p. 197, ll. 3–8)	Evolution need not result in human beings. It can result in anything. (cf. p. 197, ll. 1–2)
How can an eye come into existence by accident? (cf. p. 197, ll. 3–4)	An eye has to evolve from sth that is like an eye. (cf. p. 197, ll. 4f.)
"[…] what is the use of half an eye?" (p. 197, l. 6)	Half an eye is better than no eye if you can get away from a predator. You can survive and multiply. (cf. p. 197, ll. 6–11)
God created human beings as the superior being on earth. (cf. p. 197, ll. 12–14)	Human beings are just animals. One day evolution will produce a better human being and we will no longer be superior or we will catch a disease or make too much pollution and may die out. (cf. p. 197, ll. 14–19)

Christopher favours the scientific point of view in the discussion on evolution because he says that people who believe in God "should think logically" (p. 196, l. 4). To Christopher, logic is very important in his life because he structures his life using logic and plans. He also likes mathematics a lot and is very good at it, which requires a logical and clearly structured way of thinking. Christopher has no access to emotions and imagination. But imagination is what you need not only to believe in God, but also to understand jokes, signs, metaphors or, for example, that a constellation of stars is called *Orion* because it looks like a hunter. Christopher cannot understand either and gains access to this world only by applying logic and relying on facts.

Die Erklärungen, die Christopher in seinen Ausführungen liefert, spiegeln die aktuelle Diskussion zur *creation-evolution controversy* wider. Zur Festigung können die konträren Positionen anhand eines Arbeitsblattes gegenübergestellt werden *(Copy 17)*.

Answers to *Copy 17*: 1b/2e/3f/4a/5c/6d – alternatively: 1c/2e/3f/4a/5b/6d

Darwin versus the Bible

Darwin's theory of evolution contains several ideas that do not correspond to what the Bible says about the origin of life.
Dr. Michael Shermer, a member of the *American Sceptics Society,* contrasts Darwin with the Bible:

Match what Darwin's ideas say to what the Bible says about the same aspects.[1]

DARWIN	**THE BIBLE**
1. The world is not static but evolving (changing). Living things reproduce and change into different things.	a) "The fool hath said in his heart, There is no God." (*Psalm* 14:1)
2. God did not create things, but they arose through natural processes. Things reproduce after their kind.	b) "And God said, Let the earth bring forth grass [...] And the earth brought forth grass." (*Genesis* 1:11-12)
3. The existence of the universe is just a giant accident, it has no purpose.	c) "[...] all things continue as they were from the beginning of creation." (2 *Peter* 3:4)
4. God is an unnecessary hypothesis.	d) "And God said, Let us make man in our Image […] and let them have dominion over [...] every creeping thing that creepeth upon earth. [...]" (*Genesis* 1:26)
5. Present processes operating over long periods of time account for the world and everything in it.	e) "For in six days the Lord made heaven and earth, the sea, and all that in them Is […]" (*Exodus* 20:11)
6. Man is just an animal; man is nothing special, but just another accident of evolution with no ultimate purpose.	f) "The heavens declare the glory of God; and the firmament sheweth his handywork." (*Psalm* 19:1)

[1] cf. http://www.answersingenesis.org/creation/v17/i4/darwin.asp

4.3 Finding shelter in mother's apartment

In Kapitel 211 (S. 198ff.), 229 (S. 233ff.) und 233 (S. 236ff.) wird Christopher mit dem neuen Leben seiner Mutter konfrontiert und muss erfahren, dass die herkömmlichen Kriterien hier offenbar nicht mehr anwendbar sind und er sich neu orientieren muss. In Form eines *close readings* (Kapitel 233, S. 236–242) sollen sich die Schülerinnen und Schüler mit folgender Fragestellung beschäftigen:

Where can you see that Christopher's former arrangements for creating order in his life do not work any more? Quote from the text.
Explain what this change means for Christopher and his future life?

passages	their meaning
"I went out onto the balcony to find out whether I could see any stars, but there weren't any because of all the clouds and what is called *light pollution,* which is light from streetlights and car headlights [...] getting in the way of light from the stars." (p. 238, ll. 11–16)	Christopher cannot see the stars in the sky that were a constant element in his life and reminded him of his aims. Therefore, he cannot reach for the stars anymore and loses all hope of becoming an astronaut one day. With the stars gone, his stability in life has gone as well and it is hard for him to get a grip on his current situation. symbolic meaning: cf. the meaning of the stars in navigation (orientation)
"And the next morning I looked out of the window in the dining room to count the cars in the street to see whether it was going to be a **Quite Good Day** or a **Good Day** or a **Super Good Day** or a **Black Day**, but it wasn't like being on the bus to school [...] so the system didn't work anymore." (p. 241, ll. 3–11)	He is not even able to tell if the day will be a good or bad day, because in London, his system of counting red or yellow cars does not work any more. So everything he used to rely on to help him structure his life has gone. He must find himself a new way to get along in life but that requires self-confidence and the ability to adapt to new situations.
"Father came back to the house and I screamed [...] I went into the garden and lay down and looked at the stars in the sky and made myself negligible." (p. 248, ll. 15–18) On a previous occasion, Christopher had used very similar words: "[...] and if you have difficult things in your life it is nice to think that they are what is called *negligible* [...]" (p. 154, ll. 19–20)	Christopher feels like disappearing when his father arrives, he would have preferred not to be confronted with him again.

Da der Leser bisher wenig über die Beziehung von Mrs Boone zu ihrem neuen Lebensgefährten weiß, kann an dieser Stelle nach Hinweisen gesucht werden. Darüber hinaus stellt sich die Frage, welche Auswirkungen das Eindringen von Christopher in deren Zweisamkeit bedeutet. Diese Aufgabe kann mündlich oder schriftlich anhand von folgenden Leitfragen erteilt werden:

Obviously, Christopher is not really happy about his new life.
What about his mother and her new lover? Have they found the happiness that they were looking for? Has their situation improved?
Does Christopher's arrival make any difference?

Lösungsvorschlag:

The relationship of Roger Shears and Judy Boone is obviously not altogether harmonious because right at the beginning we witness a quarrel between them as they are coming home late at night, not seeing Christopher, who is waiting outside their apartment: "'I don't care whether you thought it was funny or not […]' 'Judy, look. I'm sorry, OK […]' 'Well, perhaps you should have thought about that before you made me look like a complete idiot.'" (p. 225, ll. 3–7)
This passage proves that there is a lack of respect towards Mrs Boone.
In addition, Roger is not pleased about the idea of Christopher living with them as well, after Christopher's mother invites her son to stay as long as he likes: "'What's he going to do? […] It's bloody ridiculous.'" (p. 236, ll. 10–11) Mrs Boone enforces her invitation, regardless of Mr Shears's complaints. This adds another burden to the relationship between Christopher's mother and her new lover. Later, Mr Shears brings Christopher books about science from the library, but unfortunately, they are for children and not interesting for Christopher at all. Even though this could be seen as an act of goodwill on the part of Roger, it shows that he is not really interested in Christopher. Despite this, Roger is angry about Christopher's reaction to his efforts. This provides another challenge for his relationship with Mrs Boone.
Christopher tries to exclude himself from this trouble by blocking it out with the sound of white noise from the radio: "And when Mother and Mr Shears argued I took the little radio from the kitchen […] and I couldn't hear Mother and Mr Shears arguing […]" (p. 242, ll. 6ff.).

Christopher kann folglich den Streit der Erwachsenen nicht weiter verfolgen. Diese Leerstelle können die Schüler füllen:

When Mrs Boone and Mr Shears start arguing Christopher turns up the volume of the radio to listen to "white noise".
Imagine what they are talking about. Write a little scene with dialogues.

Möglicher Lösungsvorschlag:

Roger enters the kitchen and puts three science books on the table for Christopher to read. Christopher looks at the titles, but puts the books aside.

R.: "Well, it's nice to know my contribution is appreciated."

J.: "But Roger, those are children's books. You should have looked at the titles. Had you ever had a child of your own, you'd know that. What do you expect? I should have asked you to bring more demanding books for Christopher. He is really clever when it comes to science. It's really amazing how much he understands. More than many grown-ups. I remember …

R.: (interrupts her in a sarcastic voice)
"Oh, sure! I forgot! That's why you left him and your husband, right? …"

Dieser Dialog kann von den Schülern erweitert und szenisch dargestellt werden, entweder als Hörspiel oder kurze Videosequenz. Als Vorbereitung für die Erarbeitung des *wall displays*

Finding shelter in mother's apartment sollen die Schüler die Geschehnisse in der Wohnung der Mutter in Form einer Zeitleiste zusammenfassen. Dies ist gut machbar, da zahlreiche Zeitadverbien diesen Textteil strukturieren.

Christopher's stay with his mother lasts for a little more than a week. Make a timeline of the events in his mother's apartment using the following structure:

Christopher's stay at his mother's apartment

1st day 2nd day 3rd day 4th day →

Christopher's arrival/
argument between
his mother – Mr Shears …

Lösungsvorschlag:

1st day (cf. pp. 225 ff.) **Monday**	Christopher's arrival/argument between his mother and Mr. Shears/visit from a policeman/Mr. Boone causing trouble/Christopher's favourite dream
2nd day (cf. pp. 236 ff.) **Tuesday**	another argument between his mother and Mr. Shears/buying clothes at Brent Cross shopping centre with mother/screaming fit at the store/worry about A levels/roaming the streets at night
3rd day (cf. p. 240, ll. 2 ff.) **Wednesday**	all alone in the morning/watching videos/missing having a garden
4th day (cf. p. 240, ll. 14 ff.) **Thursday**	mother loses job/mother has problems both with her former husband and her new lover/Christopher's frustration due to not being allowed to sit his A levels
5th day (cf. p. 241, ll. 10 ff.) **Friday**	red and yellow cars system not reliable any more/trip to Hampstead Heath/mother telling him he cannot sit his A levels/another screaming fit
6th day (cf. p. 241, ll. 21 ff.) **Saturday**	Roger Shears bringing the wrong books/further arguing between his mother and Mr Shears/listening to white noise on the radio to drown them out/Christopher refusing to eat
7th day [Sunday]	[not covered in the book]
8th day (cf. p. 242, ll. 15 ff.) **Monday**	Mr Shears entering Christopher's room at night and yelling at him while drunk/mother apologizes
9th day (cf. p. 242, ll. 23 ff.) **Monday**	mother and son leaving Chapter Road behind for Swindon

Anschließend kann auf dieser Grundlage das *wall display/part 2* weiterentwickelt werden:

Add relevant elements concerning Christopher's external and internal journey to the *wall display*.

Wall display/part 2: Finding shelter in mother's apartment

(re-)entrance

SWINDON

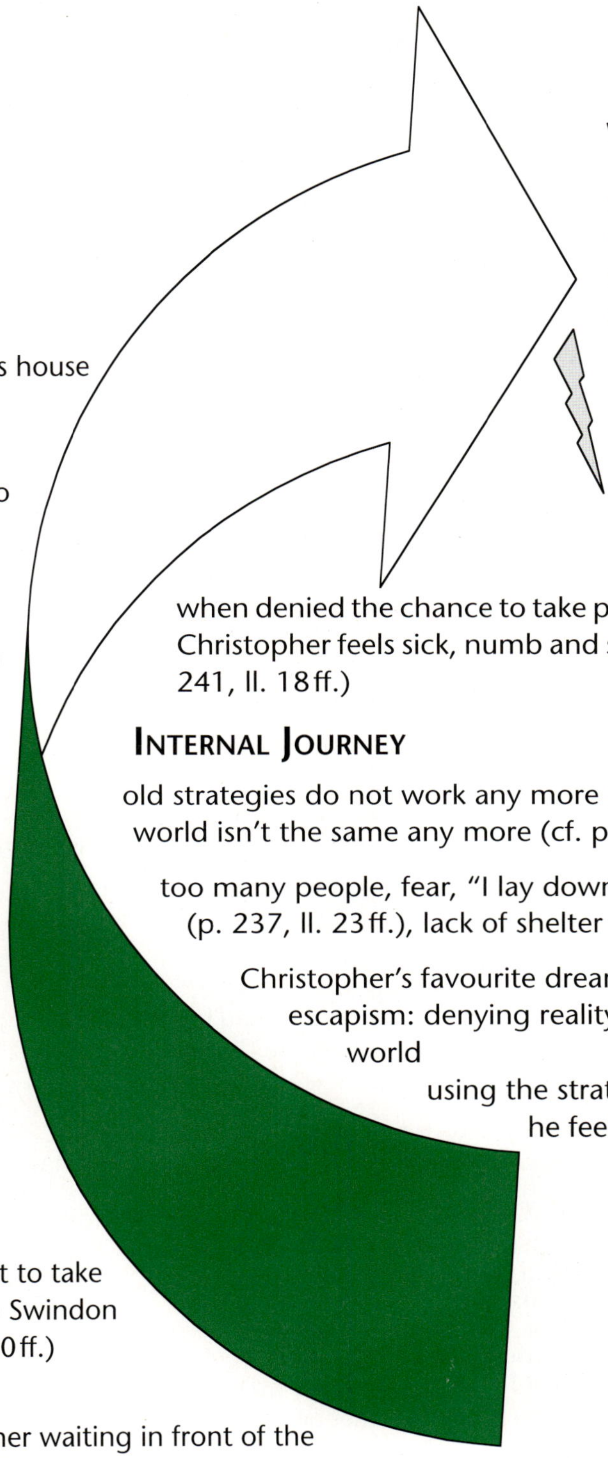

External Journey

temporary stay in father's house (cf. p. 244, ll. 4 ff.)

leaving London, return to Swindon with mother (cf. p. 243, ll. 21 ff.)

trip to Hampstead Heath (cf. p. 241, ll. 13–22)

out at night: light pollution (cf. p. 238, ll. 11–21)

trip to the shopping mall (cf. p. 236, ll. 19 ff.)

father's attempt to take his son back home fails (cf. p. 231, ll. 24 ff.)

policeman's attempt to take Christopher back to Swindon fails (cf. p. 229, ll. 20 ff.)

Christopher waiting in front of the apartment for his mother (cf. p. 224, ll. 14 ff.)

when denied the chance to take part in the maths exam, Christopher feels sick, numb and starts screaming (cf. p. 241, ll. 18 ff.)

Internal Journey

old strategies do not work any more (red and yellow cars) his world isn't the same any more (cf. p. 241, ll. 3 ff.)

too many people, fear, "I lay down [...] and I screamed" (p. 237, ll. 23 ff.), lack of shelter

Christopher's favourite dream (cf. pp. 233 ff.)

escapism: denying reality by fleeing to his dream world

using the strategy of drawing a map, he feels safer (cf. p. 227, ll. 1 f.)

4.4 Future perspectives

Die folgenden Arbeitsschritte beziehen sich auf Kapitel 233 (S. 236–256). Bevor das *wall display/part 3: Future perspectives* vervollständigt wird, sollen die Schüler Christophers Situation beim Wiedereintritt *(re-entrance)* in sein Leben in Swindon erfassen. Hierzu empfiehlt sich ein Vergleich zwischen seiner jetzigen Situation und der Ausgangssituation, ehe er durch die Geständnisse seines Vaters gezwungen wurde, seinen alten Lebensweg zu verlassen.

On the surface, Christopher is right back where he started his journey. Is his present situation comparable to his past situation, namely his situation before he was confronted with his father's confession?

Die Schülerinnen und Schüler sollen erkennen, dass sich für Christopher zunächst scheinbar nicht viel verbessert hat. Er lebt wieder im Hause seines Vaters, doch fürchtet er sich vor ihm. Christophers Hoffnung, nun doch seine Prüfung in Mathematik ablegen zu können, wird von seiner Mutter dadurch zunichte gemacht, dass sie den Prüfungstermin abgesagt hat. Dieses Gefühl der Enttäuschung ruft bei Christopher physische Schmerzen hervor. Er kann Enttäuschung nicht anders zum Ausdruck bringen: "And my chest began hurting [...] and it was like pressing your thumbnail against a radiator when it's really hot and the pain starts and it makes you want to cry and the pain keeps hurting even when you take your thumb away from the radiator." (p. 245, ll. 7–18)
Auch die Mutter ist nach Swindon zurückgekehrt. Ein Vergleich ihrer Situation mit der des Sohnes ist denkbar.

How is the mother received in Swindon? Have a look at people's reactions. Who is better off upon their return, Christopher or his mother?

passages	their meaning
"And then she made a loud wailing noise [...] I didn't like her doing this because it was a loud noise. [...] And then she said, 'Christopher, let me hold your hand. Just for once. Just for me. Will you?' [...] And I said, 'I don't like people holding my hand.'" (p. 228, ll. 10–22)	Mrs Boone is desperate, she badly needs consolation and support, which Christopher is not able to give to her.
"And father shouted, 'Is your fucking fancy man here as well?'" (p. 244, ll. 17–18)	The father's attitude towards his wife's adultery has not changed.
"Mrs Shears came across the road and said to Mother, 'You've got a fucking nerve. [...] So, has he finally dumped you, too?'" (p. 245, ll. 23–27)	Mrs Shears is also angry at her/malicious joy.
"Mr Shears was in the taxi and he got out of the taxi and threw a big cardboard box of things belonging to Mother onto the lawn." (p. 249, ll. 2ff.)	Mr Shears is upset as well.

<u>to sum up</u>: none of the people who are or used to be close to Mrs Boone support her; her life is in shambles: broken marriage, broken relationship, unfriendly neighbourhood, unemployment, handicapped son, no money, distress causes depression (requires medical treatment)

Im Gegensatz dazu (vgl. ab S. 245) wendet sich Christophers Leben zum Positiven, was von den Schülern abschließend im *wall display/part 3: Future perspectives* dargestellt werden soll.

Wall display/part 3: Future perspectives

(re-)entrance

External Journey

sits his A level (cf. p. 247, ll. 19 ff.)

lives in a flat with mother, she finds new work, but takes pills against her depression (cf. p. 251, ll. 17–20)

she gives him a puzzle (cf. p. 252, ll. 7–8)

Toby dies (cf. p. 253, l. 4)

project with his father (cf. p. 254, ll. 1 ff.)

he gets a little dog from his father (cf. p. 254, ll. 25 ff.), a lightning bolt knocks down the tree near his father's house (cf. p. 255, ll. 15 ff.)

gets an A in his maths exam (cf. p. 255, ll. 20 f.)

grows vegetables with his father (cf. p. 256, ll. 7 ff.)

S
W
I
N
D
O
N

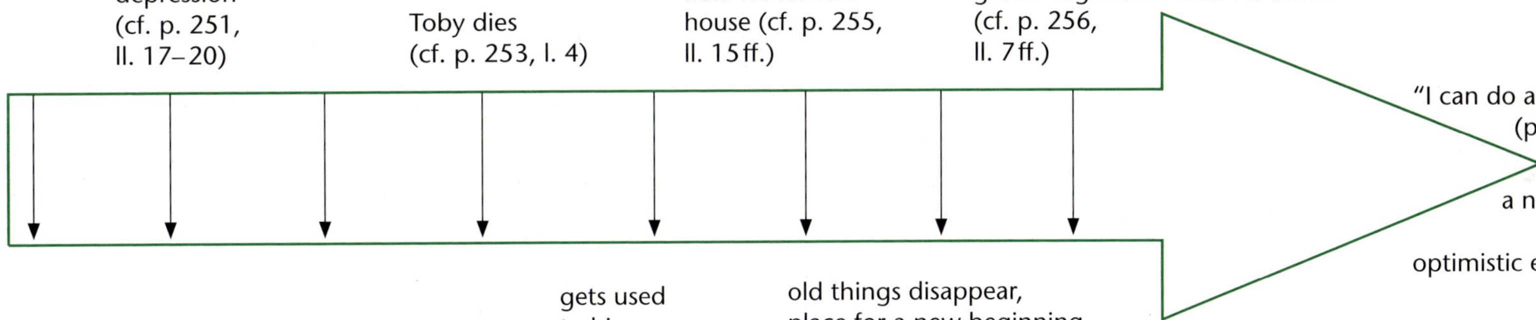

"I can do anything." (p. 256, l. 24)

a new start

optimistic ending ☺

regains control over his life

he solves the mystery

"everything was OK" (p. 251, l. 17)
"But there were more bad things than good things." (p. 252, l. 16)

gets used to his father

he's "going to pick and eat" the vegetables when they're ready (cf. p. 256, l. 8)

old things disappear, place for a new beginning

makes future plans (cf. p. 256, ll. 10 ff.)

Internal Journey

Das Ende eines alten und der Beginn eines neuen Lebensabschnittes werden durch Symbole verstärkt:

What other clues are there on pp. 253–256 which emphasize the end of something and the beginning of something new?

symbols of the end of something	symbols of a new beginning
	Mother and son paint mother's room in "White with a Hint of Wheat" (p. 252, ll. 11f.).
Toby, Christopher's rat and companion during his journey, dies. (cf. p. 253, l. 4)	His father gives him a new pet, a baby dog. (cf. p. 254, l. 25)
A lightning bolt knocks down a tree near his father's house; all that is left is a black pointed stump. (cf. p. 255, ll. 15ff.)	His father makes a vegetable patch where they can grow vegetables together; Christopher can pick and eat them when they are ready. (cf. p. 256, ll. 8f.)

to sum up:
Sometimes we are forced to give up our old habits *(ideas, way of life,* etc.). This is often hard to bear, especially when we considered these things to be the foundations of our life. At the same time, change offers the opportunity to let go of these old things. The new space that is left opens our minds and gives us the chance of a better life. When something old vanishes *(tree, Toby),* something new *(vegetables, baby dog)* can appear and develop.

Im Anschluss können den Schülerinnen und Schülern drei Aussagen des Autors Mark Haddon auf Folie kopiert präsentiert und dann diskutiert werden:

Comment on Mark Haddon's statements.
What might he mean when he says that there is something wrong with the people around Christopher?

"By the end of the book, although he hasn't profoundly changed – in a way, he hasn't changed at all – he has managed to restore order to his life. From his perspective, that's been a victory."

There "is a very true sense in which there is something more wrong with the people around Christopher than with him."

"But if you look at the people around him, they're still struggling with these huge problems. Their story is going to go on. They're the people who in some sense have something wrong with them."

Mark Haddon[1]

[1] *The Curiously Irresistible Literary Debut of Mark Haddon,* Interview with Mark Haddon from June 24, 2003 by Dave Welsh

Probleme der Menschen um Christopher werden stellenweise anhand von deren Wortwahl deutlich. Im Folgenden einige Beispiele, die sich erweitern ließen. Hier zeigt sich in vielerlei Hinsicht, dass die Menschen um Christopher stark durch ihre Emotionalität geleitet werden. Das äußert sich zum Beispiel in ihrer Wortwahl.

Examples of expletives used in the novel	
"without you shitting" (p. 57, l. 9)/"holy fucking Jesus" (p. 99, l. 23)/"bloody" (p. 100, l. 10)/"fuck" (p. 100, l. 1; p. 139, l. 19)/"I need a fucking drink" (p. 102, l. 8)/"shit" (p. 139, ll. 20f.)/"How the fuck did you get in here?" (p. 244, l. 14)/"Is your fucking fancy man here as well?" (p. 244, ll. 17f.)	Mr Boone
"What the hell is going on?" (p. 255, l. 18)/"Jumpin Jack Christ" (p. 226, l. 18)/"It's bloody ridiculous" (p. 236, l. 11)	Mr Shears
"fuck's name" (p. 8, l. 10)/"fucking dog" (p. 8, l. 15)	Mrs Shears
"shitting fuck" (p. 190, l. 27)/"bloody" (p. 191, l. 16)	policeman
"thanks a fucking bundle. Jesus [...] Oh shit." (p. 216, l. 23)/"mad as a fucking hatter. Jesus" (p. 218, l. 1–2)	man with the green raincoat
"You're fucking weird, mate." (p. 199, ll. 9f.)/"bloody nuts" (p. 199, ll. 22f.)/"daft cunt" (p. 199, l. 23)	people on the train
"suck my cock" (p. 218, l. 18)	inscription on the Tube

Diese spontanen Gefühlsausbrüche kommen von Menschen in Christophers Umfeld, nicht von ihm selbst. Zu den wenigen Personen, die neben Christophers Mutter keine Kraftausdrücke verwenden, zählt seine Therapeutin Siobhan: Sie erfüllt in vielerlei Hinsicht eine wichtige Funktion in Christophers Leben und kann als seine Mentorin *(mental guide)* auf seinem Lebensweg gesehen werden. Ihre Rolle kann in einer Hausaufgabe zusammengefasst werden:

Siobhan can be seen as Christopher's main mentor on his journey to adolescence. To what extent does Siobhan help Christopher to find his way in life?
Give examples and explain Siobhan's role.

Lösungsvorschläge:

Siobhan

- has known him for eight years (cf. p. 6, l. 3)
- gives him advice on how to write a book (cf. p. 9, ll. 2f., p. 9, ll. 17f., p. 82, ll. 26ff., p. 210, ll. 1f.)
- reads the first pages of his book (cf. p. 9, ll. 21ff.)
- is accepted by Christopher as being trustworthy (cf. p. 98, ll. 3ff.)
- cares for his well-being (cf. p. 112, ll. 7–15, p. 246, ll. 1–3)
- gives him direction (cf. p. 163, ll. 18–19)
- gives him strategies to solve problems and regain control over himself (cf. p. 164, ll. 15–19, p. 169, ll. 26–27)
- helps him to understand other people's ideas and thoughts (p. 169, ll. 26–27, p. 210, ll. 21f.)
- supports and helps him to achieve his aims (cf. p. 246, ll. 9–14)
- offers him alternatives, does not force him to do things (cf. p. 250, ll. 1ff.)

- tells him not to worry about the future but to think instead about the good things and aims which he has already achieved (cf. p. 252, ll. 3–6)

It is important that Siobhan is allowed to help Christopher with his book, because she influences Christopher's development. Her criticism and encouragement is decisive for Christopher's process of growing up. The book plays an important role because it reflects the challenges that Christopher had to go through. Writing things down helps Christopher to solve the mystery of who killed Wellington, find his mother in London and to regain control over his life.

4.5 The symbolic significance of the name "Christopher"

Obwohl Mark Haddon in einem Interview erwähnte, dass er den Namen „Christopher" nicht aufgrund etwaiger Parallelen zur Figur des heiligen Christopherus gewählt hat, so zeigen sich dennoch einige Überschneidungen:
In Kapitel 29 geht Christopher auf die Bedeutung seines Namens ein. "My name is a metaphor [...] it was the name given to St. Christopher because he carried Jesus Christ across a river [...] I do not want my name to mean a story about being kind and helpful. I want my name to mean me." (p. 23, ll. 21f.)
Die Bedeutung des Namens „Christopher" leitet sich vom griechischen Wort *christophoros* (= der Christus trägt) ab. Der heilige Christopherus gilt als Schutzpatron der Reisenden und soll im 3. Jh. n. Chr. gelebt haben.
Im Unterricht bietet es sich an, die Schüler als Hausaufgabe eine Recherche zur Namensherkunft vorbereiten zu lassen. Die Ergebnisse werden in der folgenden Stunde vorgestellt und an der Tafel festgehalten.

Here are some facts[1] about Saint Christopher.
Where can you see parallels to the figure of Christopher in the book?
Cut out the statements which could be related to Christopher and explain why.

Saint Christopher is a saint listed as a martyr from the reign of the 3rd century Roman emperor Decius.

Christopher is the patron saint of transportation and long journeys.

Saint Christopher is sometimes represented with the head of a dog. The practice of the time was to describe all people outside the "civilized" world (Greco-Roman-Persian) as dog-headed.

Jesus Christ told him to plant his staff in the ground. The staff miraculously bloomed into a fruit-bearing tree.

[1] http://en.wikipedia.org/wiki/Saint_Christopher

After he carried Jesus Christ across the river, he was baptised and acquired his name *Christopher* (= "Christ-carrier").

Before he was baptised Christopher, his name was *Reprobus* (= wicked person). His baptism to *Christopher* represents the process of changing from a lower to an enlightened person.

Lösungsvorschläge:

Christopher undergoes the process of changing from childhood to adolescence. After his journey, he looks into his future with hope and increased self-esteem.

Christopher grows vegetables with his father and plans to pick and eat them when they're ready. (→ a lightning bolt knocked down the old tree near his father's house)

Before he was baptised Christopher, his name was *Reprobus* (= wicked person). His baptism to *Christopher* represents the process of changing from a lower to an enlightened person.

Jesus Christ told him to plant his staff in the ground. The staff miraculously bloomed into a fruit-bearing tree.

The symbolic significance of the name "Christopher"

Christopher is the patron saint of transportation and long journeys.

Saint Christopher is sometimes represented with the head of a dog. The practice of the time was to describe all people outside the "civilized" world (Greco-Roman-Persian) as dog-headed.

Christopher goes on a long journey physically to London and figuratively to adolescence. (→ *story of initiation)*

Christopher likes dogs more than people. Due to his *Asperger's*, other – "civilized" – people treat him differently and often rudely, e.g. by calling him names, such as "spazzer", as if he did not belong to their world.

Component 5

Final reflections on the novel as a whole

Durch die Konzentration auf analytische Textarbeit kann möglicherweise das Gefühl für den Roman als Ganzes verloren gehen. Daher erfolgt abschließend eine ganzheitliche Betrachtung.

5.1 The symbolic significance of dogs in Christopher's story

Wie der Titel des Romans bereits andeutet, kommt Hunden in der Erzählung eine leitmotivische Bedeutung zu. Anfang und Ende des Buches entsprechen der Entwicklung Christophers. Der Romananfang (toter Hund, verhaltensauffälliger Jugendlicher mit autistischen Zügen, der auf die Hilfe anderer angewiesen ist) steht in krassem Gegensatz zum Ende des Romans (junger Hund; Christopher, der bewiesen hat, dass er trotz Behinderung sein Leben weitgehend selbst in die Hand nehmen kann). Dadurch erhält der Roman eine Kreisstruktur.
Hinweise auf Hunde sind darüber hinaus ein wiederkehrendes Motiv dieses Romans.
Mithilfe des Titelbildes und entsprechender Fragen soll auf die Bedeutung von Hunden hingewiesen werden:

Have a look at the title page. What does it hint at?
Where in the story do dogs turn up? What for?

Der anschließend kopierte Arbeitsauftrag erleichtert die Textarbeit:

DOGS – Their features and relevance for the novel

Read the following passages on dogs again and take notes.
Explain their function (with regard to Christopher and the development of the novel).

Wellington	**Ivor**	**The Hound of the Baskervilles**	**Sandy**
cf. pp. 5f.	cf. pp. 51, 70, 72	cf. pp. 86ff.	cf. pp. 254–255

Then, read the following quotes and take notes.
Identify their contexts and their meaning.

- "Best to let sleeping dogs lie" (p. 82, l. 24)
- "The dhole is *the Indian wild dog* and it looks like a fox." (p. 108, annotation)
- "that bloody dog [...] some stupid mutt" (p. 148, ll. 8ff.)
- "I made a noise like a dog barking" (p. 205, ll. 24f.)

- "I was moaning [...] like a dog, when it has hurt its paw" (p. 208, ll. 22f.)
- sticker on the guitar case saying "howl records" (cf. p. 217)
- Title "The Curious Incident of the Dog in the Night-Time"

Zu erwarten sind folgende Lösungen:

Wellington

- Mrs Shears's poodle
- murdered at the beginning of the story
- trigger for the detective story
- solution to the murder becomes the trigger for the initiation story
- drives father and son apart
- death = symbol of end (a part of Christopher's old life has to be given up)
- (historical name: Duke of Wellington, one of the leading military and political figures of the 19th century, rose to prominence in the Napoleonic Wars, victor at the Battle of Waterloo/place name: capital of New Zealand)

Ivor

- Mrs Alexander's dachshund
- the existence of this dog is reason for Christopher to trust in Mrs Alexander rather than see her as a potential stranger danger (cf. p. 51, l. 6)
- the next time he sees her, he even pets the dog and "it licked [...] [his] hand" (p. 70, l. 5), Christopher is not even disgusted at Ivor's poo (even though brown is his most hated colour, cf. p. 104)
- the dog bridges the gap between the old lady and the boy

The Hound of the Baskervilles

- title of Christopher's favourite book by Sir Arthur Conan Doyle
- a real monster (cf. p. 89, ll. 1f.)
- parallel to Wellington, the Hound of the Baskervilles is killed (cf. p. 87, l. 13f.)

Sandy

- Christopher's own pet, a golden retriever, only two months old, which he is allowed to name
- present from his father, partly to make up for the loss of Toby, his rat/reconciles father and son (cf. p. 254, ll. 25f.)
- Christopher makes friends with the dog right away and is responsible for it (cf. p. 255, l. 7, l. 11, p. 256, ll. 4f.)
- the importance of the dog is made clear when he starts to plan his future at the very end of the book: "And I can take Sandy and my books and my computer." (p. 256, ll. 29f.)
- new life = symbol of beginning/Christopher has only just begun to have his own life, like the puppy he has already had to and will have to learn many things but he is confident that he will be able to make it: "I can do anything." (p. 256, l. 24)
- circular structure of the story: beginning and end are similar (story starts and ends with a dog), but optimistic tone at the end
- affectionate name, referring to the appearance of this puppy

"Best to let sleeping dogs lie"	• proverb • typical of Mr Boone's way of thinking, particularly with regard to Christopher's detecting activities
"The dhole is the Indian wild dog and it looks like a fox."	• example of Christopher's interest in special/expert knowledge, this time carnivorous animals, mammals
"that bloody dog [...] some stupid mutt"	• swearword "bloody" and derogative term "mutt" for "dog" illustrate the father's state of mind after his confession
"I made a noise like a dog barking"	• Christopher's attempt at defending himself, dealing with people coming too close
I was moaning [...] like a dog, when it has hurt its paw"	• Christopher cannot express his innermost feelings any better, he is distressed
sticker on the guitar case saying "howl records"	• friendly lady at the tube station wants to help him after he has almost been run over by a train approaching
Title	• first hint at the relevance of dogs for this story • quote from *Silver Blaze,* another of Sir Conan Doyle's Sherlock Holmes stories (The kidnapper of a prize racehorse is found to be its own trainer. To Holmes, the clincher is "the curious incident of the night-time", which Inspector Gregory fails to understand: "The dog did nothing in the night-time." Holmes answers that exactly this "was the curious incident". – All in all, the title is somehow convoluted.) • recurring dog motive/provides the story with a frame

5.2 Memory box

Zum Abschluss der Lektüre werden Karteikarten ausgeteilt. In einer Stillarbeitsphase oder alternativ als Hausaufgabe sollen anonym Bemerkungen – z. B. Eindrücke, Kritik, interessanteste Textstelle, Spekulationen über Christophers weiteres Leben etc. – notiert werden. Die Karteikarten werden in einer Box gesammelt. Dann zieht jede Schülerin und jeder Schüler eine Karte und äußert sich zu der vorgetragenen Bemerkung. Alle sind zur Stellungnahme aufgefordert, sodass eine facettenreiche Diskussion über das Buch angeregt wird. Bei starken Lerngruppen kann die Moderatorenrolle von Schülerseite übernommen werden.

Write your final comments, such as impressions, criticism, your favourite passages, ideas with regard to Christopher's further life or any other interesting thoughts on these index cards. They will be collected, read out in class anonymously, then commented on and discussed.

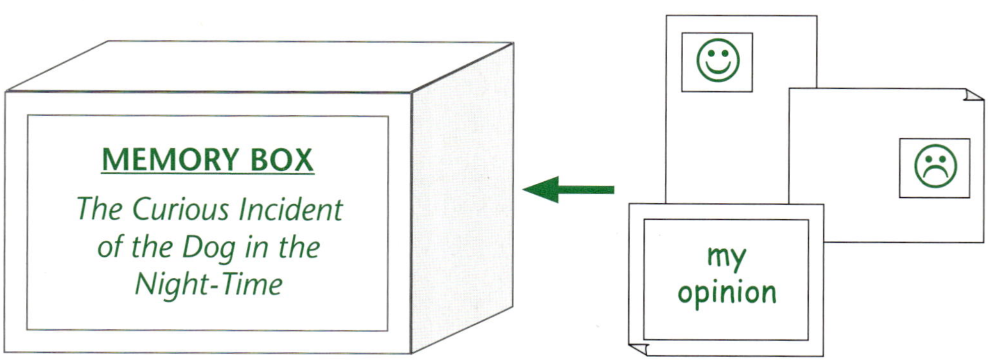

5.3 Curing *autism* desirable or not?

Die Auszüge aus einem Artikel der *New York Times* ergänzen Haddons Buch perfekt *(Copy 18)*. Die zitierten Jugendlichen sind zwei männliche Teenager mit *Asperger*-Symptomen im Alter von Christopher. Beide sind Zehntklässler der sogenannten *ASPIE School,* einer im Jahr 2003 im Staate New York neu gegründeten Ganztagschule, deren Zielgruppe Schüler mit *Asperger-Syndrom* und sog. hochfunktionalem *Autismus* – engl.: *high functioning autism (HFA)* – sind. Beide wehren sich gegen die gängige Vorstellung, sie litten an einer Krankheit, die es zu therapieren gelte. Ihr Leiden sei vielmehr in der Reaktion der Umwelt auf sie begründet. In dieser Hinsicht ist die *ASPIE School* ein Beispiel für die auch von *autistischen* Erwachsenen erhobene Forderung, statt einer ohnehin sinnlosen Therapie das Positive ihrer besonderen Persönlichkeitsmerkmale, etwa Detailgenauigkeit und Innovationsgabe, zu verstärken. Hingegen befürchten viele Eltern von *autistischen* Kindern, dass wertvolle Möglichkeiten, ihre Kinder in ein normales Leben zu integrieren, durch solche Bestrebungen verloren gehen. Sie wünschen ausdrücklich eine Therapie. Das Zitat einer Expertin am Ende des gewählten Auszuges weist darauf hin, dass man zwischen niedrigfunktionalem und hochfunktionalem *Autismus* unterscheiden sollte, bevor man sich für eine Möglichkeit entscheidet.
Anschließend können Sequenzen aus dem Film *Rain Man* eingesetzt werden. Christopher und Raymond befinden sich an verschiedenen Stellen des *autistischen* Spektrums: Christopher hat bewiesen, dass er ohne permanente Hilfe recht gut zurechtkommen kann, während die Rückführung Raymonds ins Heim unerlässlich ist.
Die Einweisung in ein Heim hatte auch Christophers Mutter erwogen (vgl. S. 61, Z. 1 f.). Als Einstieg in den Text könnte man das erwähnte Zitat als Impuls an die Tafel schreiben

> "Jesus, Christopher, I am seriously considering putting you in a home."

und hinsichtlich der Reaktion Christophers darauf (am Ende des Buches) spekulieren:

> Imagine you are Christopher at the end of the novel.
> What's your reaction to the prospect of being sent to an institution?

Die Besprechung des Gesamttextes kann mithilfe der Fragen auf dem Arbeitsblatt erfolgen. Zu erwarten sind folgende Antworten:

1. ASPIE School: an acronym of "Autistic Strength, Purpose and Independence in Education" (ll. 22f.), "school for autistic teenagers" (ll. 1f.), "experimental" (l. 5), "unconventional" (l. 15)/does not aim at changing students' behavioural problems (cf. ll. 14f.) but on the contrary, encourages them to see *autism* as sth which is "O.K." (l. 16); they teach them that there are "benefits and drawbacks" (l. 24) and to be proud of their special talents (cf. ll. 18ff., ll. 2f.) thus giving "refuge" (l. 13) to students who formerly could not get along at ordinary schools
   "mainstream schools" (l. 12 – emphasis ours): here, people like Jack and Justin got to know what it is like to be "depressed from being left out and beat up all the time" (l. 11), so their experience was entirely negative only

2. parents traditionally hope for the best for their children and they are concerned that their children's future will be destroyed if they are not taught how to behave properly; they are afraid that "unpredictable, sometimes aggressive children, whose condition can take a toll on the entire family" (ll. 29 ff.) might end up in an institution (cf. ll. 27, 29)

3. "autistic activists" (l. 32 – emphasis ours) do want help (cf. l. 35) but insist that for one thing "autistic tics" (l. 34) should not be "removed" (l. 34) as this would be comparable to dissatisfactory attempts at curing left-handedness (cf. ll. 44 f.); instead, they require people's tolerance (cf. l. 38); they also claim that doing without *autism* would be a "loss" (l. 48), supporting this thesis with the hint at the most probably *autistic* inventor of hydrogen, Henry Cavendish (cf. ll. 50 f.); their conflict with worried parents is called an "online brawl" (l. 54); some parents are derided as "curebies" (l. 56) and "slaves to conformity" (l. 57), whereas the parents reproach the activists with a "typical lack of empathy" (l. 59); all in all, the conflict is very subjective and polemical

4. Lenny Schafer twice (cf. ll. 63 f., 67) points out that it is nonsensical to do without therapy no matter where sb. is on the *autistic* spectrum: big difference between *Asperger's Syndrome* and "profound and typical disabling autism" (l. 66); with regard to the latter, e.g. his own son (cf. ll. 65 f.), he would not want to renounce therapy

5. traditional view of *autism*: "as a shell" (ll. 41, 43), implying that one day a child will be able to "emerge" (l. 42), i.e. get rid of the symptoms
   more recent view: "like a skin" (l. 43), i.e. an integral part of somebody's personality

6. facts/witnesses/people's thoughts/quotations/direct speech, emotive words, elements of a report: comprehensive information on *ASPIE School*, new developments in the field of *autism* and their importance for society in general, expert opinions (cf. ll. 50 f., 64 ff.)/subjective and story-like elements, e.g. voices of the man in the street: the text is both informative and entertaining, which is typical of interpretive news stories

7. individual answers, considering both Christopher's A levels and plans for the future and emphasizing Jack's and Justin's talents (cf. "expert" l. 2; "expertise" l. 19, "specialists" l. 20, "like a living map" ll. 1 f.) in contrast to other people with more serious problems, such as inability "to use speech to communicate" (ll. 26 f.), "unpredictable" and "aggressive" (l. 30) behaviour, "violent outbursts" (l. 34)

How about not 'curing' us, some autistics are pleading

Boiceville, N.Y. – Jack Thomas, a 10th grader at a school for autistic teenagers and an expert on the nation's roadways, tore himself away from his satellite map one recent recess period to critique a television program about the search for a cure for autism.

"We don't have a disease," said Jack, echoing the opinion of the other 15 boys at the experimental Aspie school[1] here in the Catskills. "So we can't be 'cured.' This is just the way we are."

From behind his GameBoy, Justin Mulvaney, another 10th grader, objected to the program's description of people "suffering" from Asperger's syndrome, the form of autism he has.

"People don't suffer from Asperger's," Justin said. "They suffer because they're depressed from being left out and beat up all the time."

That, at least, was what happened to these students at mainstream schools before they found refuge here.

But unlike many programs for autistics, this school's program does not try to expunge the odd social behaviors that often make life so difficult for them. Its unconventional aim is to teach students that it is O.K. to "act autistic" and also how to get by in a world where it is not.

Trained in self-advocacy, students proudly recite the positive traits autism can confer, like the ability to develop uncanny expertise in an area of interest. This year's class includes specialists on supervolcanoes and medieval weaponry.

"Look at Jack," Justin pointed out. "He doesn't even need a map. He's like a living map."

The new program, whose name stands for Autistic Strength, Purpose and Independence in Education – and whose acronym is a short form of Asperger's – is rooted in a view of autism as an alternative form of brain wiring, with its own benefits and drawbacks, rather than a devastating disorder in need of curing.

It is a view supported by an increasingly vocal group of adult autistics, including some who cannot use speech to communicate and have been institutionalized because of their condition. But it is causing consternation among many parents whose greatest hope is to avoid that very future for their children. Many believe that intensive behavioral therapy offers the only rescue from the task of caring for unpredictable, sometimes aggressive children, whose condition can take a toll on the entire family.

The autistic activists say they want help, too, but would be far better off learning to use their autistic strengths to cope with their autistic impairments rather than pretending that either can be removed. Some autistic tics, like repetitive rocking and violent outbursts, they say, could be modulated more easily if an effort were made to understand their underlying message, rather than trying to train them away. Other traits, like difficulty with eye contact, with grasping humor or with breaking from routines, might not require such huge corrective efforts on their part if people were simply more tolerant.

[...] A neurological condition that can render standard forms of communication like tone of voice, facial expression and even spoken language unnatural and difficult to master, autism has traditionally been seen as a shell from which a normal child might one day emerge. But some advocates contend that autism is an integral part of their identities, much more like a skin than a shell, and not one they care to shed.

The effort to cure autism, they say, is not like curing cancer, but like the efforts of a previous age to cure left-handedness. Some worry that in addition to troublesome interventions, the ultimate cure will be a genetic test to prevent autistic children from being born.

---

[1] **ASPIE School**: opened its doors in 2003; founded and directed by Valerie Paradiz, PhD, it swiftly became a respected national model for the education and social development of high-functioning students on the *autism* spectrum; from Fall 2006 located in Kingston, NY as a private school for students grades 7–12 (cf. http://www.aspieschool.org/aspieschool/school.htm)

That would be a loss, they say, not just for social tolerance but because autistics, with their obsessive attention to detail and eccentric perspective, can provide valuable insight and innovation. The neurologist Oliver Sacks, for instance, contends that Henry Cavendish, the 18th-century chemist who discovered hydrogen, was most likely autistic. [...] For many parents, however, the autistic self-advocacy movement often sounds like a threat to the brighter future they envision for their children. In recent months, the long-simmering argument has erupted into an online brawl over the most humane way to handle an often crippling condition.

On e-mail lists frequented by autistics, some parents are derided as "curebies" and portrayed as slaves to conformity, so anxious for their children to appear normal that they cannot respect their way of communicating. Parents argue that their antagonists are showing a typical autistic lack of empathy by suggesting that they should not try to help their children. It is only those whose diagnosis describes them as "high functioning" or having Asperger's Syndrome, they say, who are opposed to a cure.

"If those who raise their opposition to the so-called oppression of the autistic would simply substitute their usage of 'autism or autistic' with 'Asperger's,' their arguments might make some sense," Lenny Schafer, publisher of the widely circulated Schafer Autism Report, wrote in a recent e-mail message. "But I intend to cure, fix, repair, change over etc. my son and others like him of his profound and typical disabling autism into something better. Let us regain our common sense." [...]

(854 words)

by Amy Harmon, The New York Times, December 20, 2004

Content

1. Outline the concept of the ASPIE School as opposed to conventional schools.
2. State the reasons for parents' concern about this concept.
3. Summarize the recent developments in this conflict.
4. Paraphrase Lenny Schafer's point of view expressed in lines 63–68.

Form

5. Illustrate the author's use of similes to hint at the opposing approaches to *autism.*
6. Name other means used by the author to make the article attractive.

Evaluation

7. Discuss the implications of being "institutionalized" (l. 28) for Christopher, Jack and Justin.

Internetadressen

Haddons Roman

- Haddon, Mark: "B is for bestseller", Observer April 11, 2004 (http://books.guardian.co.uk/departments/childrenandteens/story/0,6000,1189538,00.html)
- Kellaway, Kate: "Autistic differences", Observer April 29, 2003 (http://books.guardian.co.uk/departments/generalfiction/story/0,6000,944097,00.html)
- Mullan, John: "Through innocent eyes", Guardian April 26, 2004 (http://books.guardian.co.uk/elements/story/0,15812,1447627,00.html)
- Mullan, John: "Expletives not deleted", Guardian May 3, 2004 (http://books.guardian.co.uk/elements/story/0,15812,1447626,00.html)
- Mullan, John: "Letters patent", Guardian May 8, 2004 (http://books.guardian.co.uk/reviewbookclub/story/0,12286,1211730,00.html)
- Mullan, John: "Funny old world", Guardian May 15, 2004 (http://books.guardian.co.uk/elements/story/0,15812,1447625,00.html)
- Weich, Dave: "The curiously irresistible debut of Mark Haddon" (www.powells.com/authors/haddon.html)

Asperger-Syndrom/Autismus

- http://www.nas.org.uk/ (Homepage der *National Autistic Society)*
- http://www.autism-society.org/site/PageServer (Homepage der *Autism Society of America)*
- http://www.autismresearchcentre.com/arc/default.asp (Homepage des *Autism Research Centre)*
- http://www.autismresearchcentre.com/research/project.asp?id=7 (Download des CAST *(= Childhood Asperger Syndrome Test* der Universität Cambridge))
- http://www.fortunecity.com/roswell/spells/260/autism.htm (hier zahlreiche Links zu weiteren relevanten Websites)
- http://www.bestbehaviour.ca/briefhistory.htm (kurze Geschichte der *Autismus*-Forschung, gut geeignet für Kurzvortrag)
- http://ani.autistics.org/dont_mourn.html (Essay „Don't mourn for us" von Jim Sinclair, eines *Autisten;* leitete 1993 eine andere Sichtweise des Phänomens *Autismus* ein)
- http://www.tonyattwood.com.au/index.htm (Leitfaden für Eltern, Lehrer, Menschen mit *Asperger-Syndrom,* beschäftigt sich mit den Unterschieden auf dem sog. "*Autismus*spektrum", z. B. niedrigfunktionaler *(low functioning autism)* und hochfunktionaler *(high functioning autism) Autismus*

Monty Hall Problem

- http://math.cofc.edu/faculty/kasman/MATHFICT/montyhall.html?pg=explain (Möglichkeit zur eigenen Durchführung dieses Phänomens)
- http://www.markhaddon.com/monty%20hall.htm (auf Haddons Homepage)

Spielfilme zum Thema *Autismus*/Filmanalyse

- http://www.disabilityfilms.co.uk/autismtoc.htm (Links zu Spielfilmen)
- http://jochen-lueders.de/vocab/film_analysis.pdf

Sherlock Holmes

- http://www.sherlock-holmes.co.uk/home.htm

Screenplay

- http://screenwriting.about.com/library/weekly/aa081501a.htm (Fachbegriffe und Beispiel zum Thema *Screenwriting)*

EinFach Englisch

Unterrichtsmodelle

Herausgegeben von Hans Kröger

Ausgewählte Titel der Reihe:

Bend it Like Beckham
Filmanalyse
86 S., DIN A4, geh. Best.-Nr. 041212

Cultures in Conflict?
Literature on Ethnic Relationships
115 S., DIN A4, kart. Best.-Nr. 041220
Audio-CD: ca. 74 Min. Best.-Nr. 062407
Textausgabe: 148 S. Best.-Nr. 041218

Dead Poets Society
Filmanalyse
67 S., DIN A4, geh. Best.-Nr. 041255

East is East
Filmanalyse
102 S., DIN A4, geh. Best.-Nr. 041228

Echoes of the Empire. The Mixed Voices of a Colonial Past
20th Century English Short Stories
119 S., DIN A4, kart. Best.-Nr. 041223
Audio-CD: 78 Min. Best.-Nr. 062405
Textausgabe: 168 S. Best.-Nr. 041224

Forrest Gump
Filmanalyse
66 S., DIN A4, geh. Best.-Nr. 041231

Fried Green Tomatoes
Filmanalyse
136 S., DIN A4, kart. Best.-Nr. 041244

Political Speeches
Historical & Topical Issues
127 S., DIN A4, kart. Best.-Nr. 041236
Audio-CD: 70 Min. Best.-Nr. 062409
Textausgabe: 132 S. Best.-Nr. 041234

Rabbit-Proof Fence
Filmanalyse
54 S., DIN A4, geh. Best.-Nr. 041240

Tennessee Williams: A Streetcar Named Desire
102 S., DIN A4, geh. Best.-Nr. 041238
Textausgabe: 109 S. Best.-Nr. 041192

Strange Fruit and Other Songs
Cries for Social Consciousness and Civil Rights
59 S., mit Audio-CD,
DIN A4, geh. Best.-Nr. 041246

Urban Poetry
84 S., DIN A4, geh. Best.-Nr. 041232
Audio-CD: ca. 25 Min. Best.-Nr. 062413

Utopia and Dystopia
Exploring Alternative Worlds
92 S., DIN A4, kart. Best.-Nr. 041204
Textausgabe: 92 S. Best.-Nr. 041202

Paul Auster: Moon Palace
76 S., DIN A4, geh. Best.-Nr. 041226

Ray Bradbury: Fahrenheit 451
72 S., DIN A4, geh. Best.-Nr. 041214

Mark Haddon: The Curious Incident of the Dog in the Night-Time
99 S., DIN A4, kart. Best.-Nr. 041252

Lorraine Hansberry: A Raisin in the Sun
98 S., DIN A4, kart. Best.-Nr. 041241

Nick Hornby: About a Boy
inkl. Filmanalyse
93 S., DIN A4, kart. Best.-Nr. 041245

Aldous Huxley: Brave New World
93 S., DIN A4, kart. Best.-Nr. 041249

Ruth Prawer Jhabvala: Heat and Dust
87 S., DIN A4, geh. Best.-Nr. 041199

Harper Lee: To Kill a Mockingbird
108 S., DIN A4, kart. Best.-Nr. 041213

Ian McEwan: The Cement Garden
55 S., DIN A4, geh. Best.-Nr. 041251

Joyce Carol Oates: Big Mouth & Ugly Girl
84 S., DIN A4, geh. Best.-Nr. 041233

Meg Rosoff: How I Live Now
106 S., DIN A4, kart. Best.-Nr. 041253

Schöningh Verlag
Postfach 2540
33055 Paderborn

Schöningh

Fordern Sie unseren Prospekt zur kompletten Reihe an:
Informationen 0800 / 18 18 787 (freecall)
info@schoeningh.de / www.schoeningh-schulbuch.de